Lake Tahoe Community College
Learning Resources Center
So. Lake Tahoe, CA   95702

TWAYNE'S WORLD AUTHORS SERIES

A Survey of the World's Literature

Sylvia E. Bowman, Indiana University

GENERAL EDITOR

FRANCE

Maxwell A. Smith, Guerry Professor of French, Emeritus
The University of Chattanooga
Former Visiting Professor in Modern Languages
The Florida State University

EDITOR

Victor Hugo

TWAS 312

Photo courtesy of French Cultural Services

Victor Hugo

Victor Hugo

By JOHN PORTER HOUSTON

Indiana University

TWAYNE PUBLISHERS

A DIVISION OF G. K. HALL & CO., BOSTON

Library of Congress Cataloging in Publication Data

Houston, John Porter.
  Victor Hugo.

  (Twayne's world authors series, TWAS 312. France)
  Bibliography: p. 160.
  1. Hugo, Victor Marie, comte, 1802–1885.
PQ2293.H66   1975   848'.7'09   74-8729
ISBN 0-8057-2443-5

MANUFACTURED IN THE UNITED STATES OF AMERICA

Contents

About The Author

John Porter Houston was born on April 21, 1933, in Alhambra, California. He received his B.A. in 1954, from the University of California at Berkeley. In 1954–55 he studied at the Université d'Aix-Marseille and in 1959 received his Ph.D. from Yale University.

From 1958 to 1962 Dr. Houston served on the faculty of Yale University. He is currently Professor of French and Italian at Indiana University. Dr. Houston is the author of *The Design of Rimbaud's Poetry* (Yale University Press, 1963); *The Demonic Imagination: Theme and Style in French Romantic Poetry* (Louisiana State University Press, 1969); and *Fictional Technique in France 1802–1927: An Introduction* (Louisiana State University Press, 1972). He is presently involved in a study of late nineteenth-century French poets.

Preface

There has been a great revival of Hugo studies in the last decade or so. The works of Jean Gaudon, Richard B. Grant, and others, the critical editions of Léon Cellier, Pierre Albouy, René Journet, and Guy Robert all have contributed profoundly to a renewed understanding of the poet. However, there has been no general presentation of Hugo's work in English, the task which this volume attempts. Hugo is primarily known as a poet in France, and, more than anything else, this is an introduction to his poetry, including verse drama. The novels, which have been excellently analyzed in English by Grant, will be only cursorily treated, the *Théâtre en liberté*, the travel works, and the expository prose are but touched on here and there, and even within the poetry some focus and elimination has been necessary, if nothing else because of its bulk. I have quoted copiously from Hugo's verse in an attempt to guide the reader in possible future investigations, which would be highly discouraging if no stable points were suggested to begin with. Works like *Les Chansons des rues et des bois* or *L'Art d'être grand-père*, which were famous in their day, are no more than mentioned. My emphasis has been placed on the more stylistically interesting among the earlier poems and the more visionary among the later ones. The prevailing nature of present-day interest in Hugo, as exemplified in Jean Gaudon's *Choix de poèmes* (Manchester University Press, 1957), has dictated this choice.

The work this book invites comparison with is Jean-Bertrand Barrère's excellent *Hugo: L'Homme et l'Oeuvre*. Whereas Barrère has given a rather full treatment of Hugo's life, I summarize parts of it only when they seem pertinent to his *oeuvre*. (André Maurois' very readable full-scale biography is available in English.) As for the works themselves, Barrère very carefully traces the often complex genesis of each one, the biographical and literary influences upon it. I have done relatively little of this—save for the biblical influence on Hugo—in order to focus on questions of style and formal design. Barrère assumes a French public; I must assume one which has little previous knowledge of Hugo and only a limited command of

French. This brings us to the question of translations: There exists no standard or complete translation of Hugo into English, although larger libraries have sets of selected works, often anonymously translated, which were published many years ago and tend, in any case, to slight the poetry. Since Hugo's poetry is as difficult to put into English as Keats's or Shelley's is to put into French, I have tried to encourage the reader to study the verse quotations in French by appending English prose translations. Hugo's language is not so complex or obscure as that of many more recent poets, but it still offers problems of interpretation and meaning. My method, as well as my selection, will, I hope, win Hugo more readers. Unlike various other French Romantic poets, whose names, if not works, are also known outside of France, Hugo is a poet of European stature and deserves to be recognized as such.

JOHN PORTER HOUSTON

Bloomington, Indiana

Chronology

1802   Victor-Marie Hugo born in Besançon, the son of Joseph-Léopold-Sigisbert Hugo, an army officer, and Sophie-Françoise Trébuchet. Hugo has two older brothers, Abel and Eugène.

1803   The Hugo family leaves for Corsica and Elba.

1807   Madame Hugo and her children leave for Italy.

1808   Madame Hugo and her children return to Paris. Major Hugo leaves Italy for Spain.

1809   Madame Hugo is involved with an anti-Napoleonic conspirator. Major Hugo is named Count and General.

1810   Madame Hugo's lover is arrested in her house.

1811   Madame Hugo and her children leave to join the General in Spain. General Hugo asks for a divorce.

1812   The Hugos return to France.

1817   The French Academy recognizes the merit of one of Hugo's poems.

1818   The Hugos are legally separated.

1819   Two odes by Hugo receive an award from the Jeux floraux de Toulouse. First issue of the *Conservateur Littéraire* (*Literary Conservative*), founded by the Hugo brothers.

1821   Madame Hugo dies. Hugo is secretly engaged to Adèle Foucher.

1822   Publication of *Odes et Poésies diverses* (*Odes and Various Poems*). Louis XVIII grants Hugo a pension. Hugo marries Adèle Foucher. Hugo's brother Eugène becomes insane at the wedding.

1823   Publication of *Han d'Islande* (*Han of Iceland*). Louis XVIII grants Hugo a second pension.

1824   Birth of Léopoldine Hugo.

1825   Coronation of Charles X. Hugo is invited. Hugo travels in the Alps and Switzerland with Charles Nodier.

1826   *Bug-Jargal* published. *Odes et Ballades* (*Odes and Ballads*) published. Birth of Charles Hugo.

1827   Hugo meets Sainte-Beuve. *Cromwell* published.

1828   General Hugo dies. Birth of François-Victor Hugo.

1829   Publication of *Les Orientales* (*Oriental Poems*) and *Le Dernier Jour d'un condamné à mort* (*The Last Day of a Man Condemned to Death*). *Marion de Lorme* written. *Hernani* written.

1830   *Hernani* published. *Notre-Dame de Paris* (*The Cathedral of Notre Dame*) begun. Birth of Hugo's daughter Adèle.

1831   *Notre-Dame de Paris* published. First performance of *Marion de*

Lorme. Beginning of the love affair between Sainte-Beuve and Madame Adèle Hugo. *Les Feuilles d'automne* (*Autumn Leaves*) published.

1832 Hugo writes *Le Roi s'amuse* (*The King Takes His Amusement*) and *Lucrèce Borgia.* Hugo moves to the Place Royale (now the Place des Vosges and site of the Musée Victor Hugo). First performance of *Le Roi s'amuse* and suspension of the play by government censorship.

1833 First performance of *Lucrèce Borgia.* Beginning of the lifelong liason between Hugo and Juliette Drouet. *Marie Tudor* written and first performed.

1834 Publication of *Littérature et Philosophie mêlées* (*Literature and Philosophy Mingled*) (occasional essays). Hugo breaks with Sainte-Beuve. *Claude Gueux* published.

1835 *Angelo* written and first performed. Publication of *Les Chants du crépuscule* (*Songs at Daybreak*).

1837 *Les Voix intérieures* (*Inner Voices*) published. Hugo made an officer of the Légion d'Honneur. Trip to Belgium with Juliette Drouet.

1838 *Ruy Blas* written and first performed.

1839 *Les Jumeaux* (*The Twins*) begun and left unfinished. Hugo travels with Juliette to Alsace, the Rhineland, Switzerland, and Provence.

1840 *Les Rayons et les Ombres* (*Sunbeams and Shadows*) published. Trip to the Rhineland with Juliette.

1841 Hugo elected to the French Academy.

1842 *Le Rhin* (*The Rhine*) published.

1843 Léopoldine Hugo married. First performance of *Les Burgraves* (*The Burgraves*). Trip to Spain with Juliette. Léopoldine is drowned with her husband.

1844 Hugo acquires a second "official" mistress, Madame Biard.

1845 Hugo named Peer of France.

1847 Speech in the House of Peers in favor of the Bonapartes' return.

1848 Hugo attempts a speech to save the July Monarchy. Elected to the *Assemblée Constituante.* Hugo's apartment invaded during the June riots. Hugo's newspaper *L'Evénement* (*The Event*) begins publication. Speech against the death penalty.

1849 Hugo elected to the Legislative Assembly. Speech on poverty. Speech on papacy which brings about his break with the Right.

1850 Speeches against education being in the hands of the Church, deportation, and speeches in favor of universal suffrage and freedom of the press.

1851 Hugo continues to oppose the Government. Goes into hiding and then exiled after the coup d'état.

1852 Official expulsion from France. Hugo writes *Histoire d'un crime* (*Story of a Crime*) and *Napoléon le petit* (*Napoleon the Little*). Hugo moves from Belgium to Jersey.

Chronology

for the supporters of the Commune. *Depuis l'exil* (*Since Exile*) published.
1877 *La Légende des siècles* (*Deuxième Série*) published. *L'Art d'être grand-père* (*The Art of Being a Grandfather*) published. *Histoire d'un crime* published to ward off an anticipated Rightist coup d'état.
1878 *Le Pape* (*The Pope*) published. Hugo has a stroke and will write virtually nothing more.
1879 *La Pitié suprême* published.
1880 *Religions et Religion* (*Religions and Religion*) published. *L'Ane* published. The public is unaware that Hugo has ceased writing and is publishing works long since written.
1881 *Les Quatre Vents de l'esprit* (*The Four Winds of the Spirit*) published.
1882 *Torquemada* published.
1883 Juliette Drouet dies. *La Légende des siècles* (*Série complémentaire*) is published.
1885 Hugo dies. State funeral and burial in the Panthéon.
1886 *La Fin de Satan* published. *Le Théâtre en liberté* (*Free Plays*) published.
1888 First part of *Toute la lyre* (*The Whole Lyre*) published.
1891 *Dieu* published.
1893 Second part of *Toute la lyre* published.
1898 *Les Années funestes* (*The Fatal Years*) published.
1902 *Dernière Gerbe* (*Last Gleanings*) published.
1942 *Océan* (*Ocean*) and *Tas de pierres* (*Heap of Stones*) published.

CHAPTER 1

Beginnings

I *Childhood*

H UGO'S early years can be looked at in three ways: There are objective documents; the version of his childhood given in the *Victor Hugo raconté par un témoin de sa vie*, which, many years later (1863), the poet's wife wrote and published under his inspiration; and the psychoanalytic method which has been applied by one critic to Hugo's emotional development with remarkable results.[1] Happily, all three approaches complement each other to a satisfying degree. While Hugo did not care to reveal what he knew of his parents' difficult marriage, infidelities, and separations, his early published work reflects the conflict of loyalties between his Royalist mother and his father, whose rise in the world was dependent on the Bonapartes. The *Victor Hugo raconté* stresses the way in which certain experiences, gruesome or strange, things seen in Spain and Italy, playing in the Hugos' private garden in Paris, and the closeness of the three Hugo brothers contributed to his adult sensibility. The reverse side of the brothers' good relations, however, to take just one example, was rivalry among them, which finds expression in Hugo's work, though sometimes in covert form, just as his parents' opposing claims on him show up in ambivalent political attitudes. Hugo's benevolent conscious feelings and his corresponding hostile ones disclosed by analysis of his work coexist in a much clearer fashion than psychoanalytic readings of writers often show.

Beyond the tangled familial relations which Freudian interpretations emphasize, there is an area of sensibility where certain accidents of experience play a determining role, and here the *Victor Hugo raconté* is especially valuable. The principal event in Hugo's early years, beyond the involvement with parents and siblings, was the stay in Spain in 1811–12, when Hugo's father, in whom Joseph Bonaparte had taken an interest, was promoted to the rank of general and made a count of the new—and short-lived—Spanish monarchy established by Napoleon's brother. The Hugos lived among a hostile, secretive population, which made a great impression by its archaic obsession with nobility and religion, and by the violence with which it waged a guerrilla war against the occupying French. Although Hugo claimed he did not enjoy his life in Spain, the country was to assume enormous importance in his imagination and served as the archetype for all places foreign or medieval. He never forgot Spanish and was periodically to deepen further his knowledge of Hispanic society and history. There was much more to this than the exoticism commonplace among other Romantic writers; Spain came to embody the irrational violent forces that haunted Hugo and which he did not like to see in the progressive, rationalistic culture of nineteenth-century France. It is as if Spain had become a kind of home of the willful and sinister unconscious.

Hugo's early experiences did not find immediate full expression in his writings, since he was first to pass through the restricting conventions of French Neoclassicism in its late and more contorted phase. In fact, the first few years of his literary career can be seen as a process of bringing to the surface preoccupations which prevailing canons of taste had obscured. Of course, these years were also ones of increasing mastery of formal and stylistic resources, and we shall begin by examining his work in the light of the poetic tradition in which he learned his craft.

II Odes

Hugo's first book was a volume of odes (1822), a fact which set him apart from his most talented contemporaries, Lamartine and Vigny. The word and the notion of the ode were conservative if not already old-fashioned as a poetic concept. Ode had designated since the Renaissance the most ambitious kind of lyric poetry, generally solemn, embellished more so than any other genre with rhetorical devices, and written often in longish, sometimes complicated stanzas. The forbidding sublimity of the genre did not discourage the writing of odes, but hardly more than two or three poets of the Neoclassical period succeeded in winning any enduring fame for their efforts. The most admired poets since the later eighteenth century had not, in fact, cultivated the ode much; they preferred to write love poems, which they called elegies, or descriptive poems. Hugo admitted in the 1823 preface to his odes that the genre was generally considered cold and monotonous, but explained how he had attempted to renovate it by placing the "movement of the ode in ideas rather than in words," by which he meant pruning away the traditional superabundance of apostrophes, exclamations, and other "vehement figures," in order to focus on the possible dramatic elements in the subject matter itself. In a sense he succeeded. When we compare Hugo's first odes with those of Jean-Baptiste Rousseau and "Lebrun-Pindare," his most famous predecessors in the eighteenth century, we are dealing with sufficiently minor poetry that the modern reader may not readily feel any notable superiority in a particular poet or poem. French readers of 1822, however, were accustomed to so narrow a range in poetic vocabulary and achievement that they perceived shades of difference where we must look hard to find any. And yet a certain quality of drama comes across even in Hugo's "political" odes, which deal with the restored Bourbon royal family and public events—the most old-fashioned kind of elevated subject matter. The ode on the death of the Duc de Berry, the heir to the throne assassinated in 1820, will serve as an example of Hugo's odes at their most solemn. The Duke was killed on the festive Sunday before Ash Wednesday, which permits the poet to contrast dramatically the event and its date, the date and the remorseful morrow which is to follow. A certain degree of elliptic leaping from the funeral to the scene of the royal family at the death-bed, remembering its members lost in the Revolution, and to the scene of the assassination itself, reverses chronology for increasing vividness of the events depicted; there is, indeed, an ingenious kind of planning at work in the poem.

Although the structure of the ode on the death of the Duc de Berry is skillfully worked out, the language shows the considerable limitations of the "sublime" Neoclassical style. *Modérons les transports d'une ivresse insensée*, the poet announces at the beginning, with something less than intensity: Calming "transports" was so familiar a combination in poetic language that it was the thing automatically expected to be done with transports; that the latter are of "mad intoxication" merely adds two more endlessly employed terms of poetic diction to the phrase. In short, its banality is that of colorless words which were applied without distinction to all kinds of emotions. If derivative, circumscribed vocabulary is one flaw in Hugo's earliest style, obscurity is the other. Unlike tragedy, which is all most readers generally know of Neoclassical French poetic style, the ode was considered the appropriate genre for elaborate periphrases. The poet, calling on Paris to cease its banquets, urges the city to look toward the *cirque où l'on voit aux accords de la lyre/S'unir les prestiges des arts.* The "circus" in which the lyre's notes join art's distinction, is merely an elevated way of designating a public building, in this case a church. Lyres refer to both music and poetry; the church's interior is a product of architecture and painting, and the answer to the puzzle is that the Duke's requiem mass is taking place. Some study of subsequent lines is necessary, however, in order to reach this conclusion. The periphrasis is not beautiful, but merely in the way. Hugo's statement that he was more concerned with the idea than the word in his odes is true in a way he did not realize at the time: The style took care of itself and was to a large extent a mingling of rather worn Neoclassical expressions and devices.

Among the odes dealing with subjects which fitted the traditional notions of elevation can be found a group of religious ones in which biblical material is sometimes present. The latter anticipates the enormous role the Bible was to play in Hugo's inspiration, especially in his later years. They are relatively timid in imitating the more imagistic aspects of biblical style, in that they continue the long Neoclassical tradition of verse paraphrases of Psalms and of the prophets. (It is perhaps not always sufficiently realized how important biblical inspiration was in French poetry up to and through the Romantic period.) However, the prophetic or apocalyptic tone attracted Hugo, and, at its most successful, helped to break through the stereotyped diction inherited from the eighteenth century. Here is an especially striking example from "L'Antéchrist":

> *Il viendra,—quand l'orgueil, et le crime et la haine*
> *De l'antique alliance auront enfreint le voeu;*
> *Quand les peuples verront, craignant leur fin prochaine,*
> *Du monde décrépit se détacher la chaîne;*
> *Les astres se heurter dans leurs chemins de feu;*
> *Et dans le ciel,—ainsi qu'en ses salles oisives*
> *Un hôte se promène, attendant ses convives,—*
> *Passer et repasser l'ombre immense de Dieu.*

(He [the Antichrist] will come, when pride, crime, and hate have broken the vow of the ancient covenant; when all nations will see, fearing their near end, the bonds of the crumbling world undone, the planets collide in their fiery paths, and in the sky—like a host who, waiting for his guests, wanders in his idle halls—the immense shadow of God pass and pass again.)

The simile, with its concreteness and the startling final image, contrasts sharply with the bland periphrasis designating the planets' orbits and the wordy way of saying "man has broken the covenant." The Bible was for Hugo as much an introduction to a new kind of style—at once direct and grandiose—as it was a work of religious teaching in any narrow sense of the term, for there is nothing doctrinal in his poetry. Unbaptized and raised by a Voltairean mother, Hugo's short period of Catholicism in the 1820's is indistinguishable from the literary influence of Chateaubriand, who, in *Le Génie du christianisme* (*The Genius of Christianity*, 1802), had succeeded in dissolving the theological core of Christianity in a tincture of aestheticism: Christian art, to which he annexed the whole of the Bible, was superior to pagan. The stylistic implications were clearly that the deistic Neoclassicism of the eighteenth century was doubly inferior, being but a pale reflection of Greco-Roman models. This curious superposition of aesthetic taste, religion, and politics (for Chateaubriand was a Royalist) brings us to the subject of the Romantic movement in France and its peculiarities.

III *Romanticism*

The history of French polemics over Romanticism need not detain us unduly, since they were often unintelligent and today are sometimes almost unintelligible, the perspective of the participants being difficult to recapture. Suffice it to say that the prominent younger poets of the 1820's leaned toward religiosity and Catholicism, that their interest in foreign literatures (the term Romanticism had come from Germany, in the sense of a literary movement) excited chauvinism in their detractors, and that arguments about Romanticism drifted easily into extraliterary matters. Hugo and other poets of similar inclinations found it limiting and irrelevant to be called Romantic and stressed their use of the national heritage which they saw as antirevolutionary, medieval, and even folkloristic.

The real problem facing French poets was a stylistic one, and it assumed a different form from the one English and German poets had coped with in preceding decades. Whereas in England, for example, Neoclassicism had not obliterated a strong consciousness of an earlier literary tradition—notably the work of Spenser and Milton—on which the new poetry could draw, French poets had no models of such scope to inspire them in their attempt to break away from the restrictive and stereotyped patterns of Neoclassical diction. Archaism, a characteristic of some English Romantic styles, had been attempted by poets during the Empire and found artificial, and, in any case, the pre-Neoclassical French poets enjoyed only a minor prestige compared with Shakespeare or Milton. In short, French poets had to find a modernist, an innovative, solution to the problem of style. This ultimately characterized the whole history of French poetry in the nineteenth century, which consisted of successive waves of innovation through to the end of the period, something much less perceptible in Victorian England. Subject matter was initially less of a question: Anything could, if necessary, be treated in the periphrastic late Neoclassical style. The first stage in broadening the possibilities of poetic language was one of elimination of eighteenth-century stylistic mannerisms, and, slowly at first, the introduction of a wider vocabulary which, if it seems perhaps only timidly inventive today, nevertheless constituted a steady erosion of Neoclassical taste. Hugo was working at this while he was still producing odes in the traditional sublime style.

IV   *The* Ballade

In later editions of the odes, which by then had become *Odes et Ballades* (1826 and 1828), Hugo rearranged his poems so that their order was not chronological, but followed a pattern of development in style and subject. We must remember, however, that, as all through his life, he worked simultaneously in different poetic modes. First he placed the official or public odes, then, toward the end, a group of poems which do not always correspond to the Neoclassical conception of the ode. There are personal poems, a kind not excluded from the ode but shading off into lesser genres, and, most unconventional of all, such things as a poem on a bat, a nightmare, a dragonfly, and a Tahitian girl imploring her European lover not to desert her. Finally, there is the section called *Ballades*.

For the French Romantics, the ballad was to the ode what Shakespeare was to Neoclassical tragedy. The ballad used direct narrative rather than elaborate leaps from one aspect of a subject to another; thus, its drama derived from a situation rather than an artifice of arrangement. It eschewed periphrasis because its spirit was popular rather than learned, and refrains or other repeated material gave an effect of naïveté to its composition. This conception of the ballad derived, sometimes quite indirectly, from English and German sources, including both folksong and modern poems modeled on popular ones. The English contribution consisted of collections of folk poetry and Walter Scott's verse, for it must be remembered that the greatest English Romantic poetry was to remain largely unknown for many years (this was true in particular of the major English Romantic odes). From Germany came not so much folk verse as the art ballads of Bürger, Schiller, and Goethe. Some French attempts at the ballad had preceded Hugo's, but his remain the best known.

The *Ballades* have varied sources, and two use archaizing verse forms, but on the whole the collection is quite homogeneous. Coming to them after a reading of the odes, we feel that all the more obtrusive elements of traditional poetic diction have been eliminated, that the vocabulary of arms, religious life, and other important aspects of medieval culture is exact and nicely handled, and that the many first persons represent skillfully created speakers and provide a distinctly dramatic or situational quality in the poems. By the time he was working on the last ballads, Hugo was reading Ronsard and the sixteenth-century poets, whom his friend Sainte-Beuve had introduced him to, but whatever influence they may have had on him was so completely absorbed that we rarely have the feeling of pastiche or extraneous interference with the natural working out of Hugo's new manner. [2]

It is notable that with one or two exceptions Hugo was not attempting to create a voluptuous or sumptuous descriptive effect in the *Ballades*. This is especially true of the more medievally colored ones. His purpose was to suggest a quality of life and turn of mind. For example, in "La Légende de la nonne" ("The Legend of the Nun") what is important is not so much the fact that a nun fell in love with a brigand (the unprepossessing material came evidently from a Gothic novel) as the effect of the story on its contemporaries and on the speaker's audience:

> *Elle prit le voile à Tolède,*
> *Au grand soupir des gens du lieu,*
> *Comme si, quand on n'est pas laide,*
> *On avait droit d'épouser Dieu.*
> *Peu s'en fallut que ne pleurassent*
> *Les soudards et les écoliers.—*

> *Enfants, voici des boeufs qui passent,*
> *Cachez vos rouges tabliers!*

(She took the veil at Toledo, to the great sorrow of the inhabitants: as if, when you're not ugly, you had the right to marry God. Soldiers and students almost cried.—Children, bulls are passing; hide your red smocks.)

The popular-sounding expression in lines three and four and the charming refrain, with its air of genuine folksong, suggest a certain kind of audience, one as much part of the artistic illusion as the narrative. The whole story is told with appropriate commentary and rounded off by bringing its fame up to the present:

> *Cette histoire de la novice,*
> *Saint Ildefonse, abbé, voulut,*
> *Qu'afin de préserver du vice*
> *Les vierges qui font leur salut,*
> *Les prieures la racontassent*
> *Dans tous les couvents réguliers.—*
> *Enfants, voici des boeufs qui passent,*
> *Cachez vos rouges tabliers!*

(The abbot Saint Ildefonse required that this story of the novice be told by the Prioresses in all convents under rules in order to preserve from vice virgins working at their salvation.)

The somewhat turned-about word order of the last stanza represents the formality of the abbot's decree as well as demonstrating Hugo's extraordinarily supple command of syntax, which we shall have occasion to return to later.

A ballad like "La Légende de la nonne" constitutes a more determined attempt to write poetry which would be farthest from the traditional ode than Hugo would ever make afterward. Folkloric poetry was not an essential or durable part of his imagination. The *Ballades* were the last poems which Hugo was to write in a mode which others had handled and which corresponded to a clear-cut literary fashion. After their publication, furthermore, the polemics over Romantic poetry gradually assumed less importance, as it became clear that lyricism in the nineteenth century was taking its own directions and that arguments over it could only be idle.

V *Early Fiction*

Neoclassical theory has nothing to say about prose fiction, and therefore the development of the novel was not accompanied by the same kind of polemics as that of the lyric or the theater. Hugo wrote two pieces of fiction during the period of his odes, *Han d'Islande* (1823) and *Bug-Jargal* (1826). The first is a lurid historical romance in keeping with the fashion of the Gothic novel and melodrama. Although the material approaches the subliterary, it demonstrates the way in which Hugo's imagination moved in a parallel manner, encompassing a whole spectrum of tastes from the ode on down.

Han d'Islande is laid in seventeenth-century Norway and deals with a young man who, in order to restore the honor of his fiancée's father, convicted of treason, sets out to find a box containing documents which will right the situation. Ordener's quest is to take him through sinister adventures in search of the outlaw monster Han, who supposedly has the box in his possession. After a great variety of episodes involving the murderous Han, who loves only destruction and death, and various minor characters, Han surrenders to the law, kills himself, the box of documents comes to light, and Ordener marries Ethel. Considerable amounts of traditional demonic symbolism give the narrative its peculiar color.

It is impossible to convey in a résumé the multiplicity of lesser figures and episodes in the work or the disjointed, fitful way in which the story is told. For one whose sense of composition was as strong as Hugo's, the work suggests parody (of which there seems to be a distinct element) and very free improvisation. The peculiar element in the story, which is related to the fact that there is no attempt made to highlight one element of the plot at the expense of another, is that in the range of villains, the enemies of Ethel's father are far more persistent and devious than the monster Han, who, through much of the tale, seems as if, in accordance with the title, he should be the central figure of evil. His surrender and suicide make him an odd figure to find in this type of black-and-white tale, while Ordener, who is essentially passive and does not really bring about the denouement, yields in importance to Han. The work has been analyzed as a traditional romance pattern in which odd displacements of emphasis occur: Ordener's destruction of Han, toward which the story seems to tend, never occurs, and Han is free to kill himself for reasons of his own which have nothing to do with the logic of the plot.[3] He has become a counterhero, usurping the reader's interest and creating a mysterious problem where none should be. Transformations of sinister figures will later preoccupy Hugo in many of his narratives or plays. Here, in a very crude form, is a constant of his imagination.

Hugo's other early narrative, *Bug-Jargal*, is the story of a slave revolt in Santo Domingo and, while much simpler than *Han d'Islande*, is again focused on sinister adventures and figures. We shall not deal with it here because of its more commonplace nature. One remark is in order, however, about both works. The general level of fictional skill was not very high in France during the 1820's, as research into Balzac's early work and its background has shown.[4] That Hugo's first novels are not better should hardly surprise us given this fact and considering that he had as yet not conceived a serious purpose in the genre. *Notre-Dame de Paris* was to be another matter altogether.

CHAPTER 2

Pure Poetry and Inspiration from Art

I Les Orientales

B Y the time he published *Les Orientales* at the beginning of 1829, Hugo was recognized as the leader of the new school of literature and many of his characteristic traits had clearly emerged. The influence of Chateaubriand's Royalism and Catholicism had passed; with the preface to *Cromwell* (1827) a bourgeois-liberal orientation became clear in his thinking, an orientation which extended to both politics and aesthetic matters. His anti-Neoclassical stance had thus, in a sense, achieved a general coherence as he rejected legitimism after the traditional canons of literary taste. However, being bourgeois-liberal in politics does not necessarily create for a poet an audience among like-minded people, who may be arch-conservatives in art. In point of fact, Hugo's new attitude toward lyric poetry was to fuel the bohemian movement with its slogan of art for art's sake.

The preface to *Les Orientales* reflects from the beginning Hugo's association with a number of painters of his generation: "The author of this book does not recognize the critic's right to question the poet about his fantasy and to ask him why he has chosen this or that color . . ." The critic cannot object to the "colors used, but only the way they are used." There are no good or bad subjects; "everything is a possible subject; everything is in the domain of art." The theory of the autonomy of art was perhaps easier to formulate first in the field of the beaux arts, where the study of execution of subject matter had always been the artist's first concern. Neoclassical literary theory had, on the other hand, always allowed a more or less generous place to theorizing about moral purpose in the work of art, the useful joining the beautiful. Hugo specifically refers to the latter when he presents his work as a "useless book of pure poetry." We shall return later to the significance of this remark, to Hugo's scoffing at the notion of the "limits of art," but it is important to note that the theory of *l'art pour l'art* originates in the rejection of a Neoclassical way of reasoning. It is perhaps because of the

persistence of the latter that the whole complex of bohemian attitudes toward art became so sharpened so early in France.

Hugo compared his new book to an old Spanish city full of
monuments of various periods, Christian and Islamic. This analogy
is not meant to evoke clutter, but a subtle interrelation of poems
which had a timely interest, since the Greek war of independence
drawing to an end suggested Turkish subjects, which in turn were
connected with the Near East in general, with the biblical cities
of the plain, with Mazeppa, prince of the Oriental Cossacks, and,
of course, with the Arabs. The civilization of the latter spread with
the Moors into Spain and so Islam links Granada and Istanbul.
The wholeness of *Les Orientales* as a collection does not, however,
depend merely on such associations, although they are important,
but comes from stylistic tendencies running throughout the volume.
While these may be found here and there in Hugo's previous poetry,
Les Orientales constitutes nonetheless a new phase of his work.

The opening poem, "Le Feu du ciel" ("The Fire from Heaven"),
which deals with the destruction of Sodom and Gomorrah, is
ingeniously placed: No subsequent poem is biblical. It stands
apart in that respect, but the themes of death and ruin lead very
smoothly into the poems on the Greek war and the bellicose Turks.
Its length demands a commanding position, and its style presents
major characteristics of *Les Orientales*:

> La voyez-vous passer, la nuée au flanc noir?
> Tantôt pâle, tantôt rouge et splendide à voir,
> Morne comme un été stérile?
> On croit voir à la fois, sur le vent de la nuit,
> Fuir toute la fumée ardente et tout le bruit
> De l'embrasement d'une ville.

(Do you see pass by the black-flanked storm cloud? Now pale, now red,
and magnificent to see, gloomy as a sterile summer? It looks, on the night
wind, like both all the burning smoke and all the roar of a flaming city
rising up.)

The language is at once highly descriptive, as in the use of color
adjectives, and shading off into metaphoric values, such as the
comparison with an infertile hot season. The simile seems at first
to suggest the character of the inhabitants of Sodom. Then, however,
it becomes clear that Hugo is not directly concerned with the damned

cities: it is not the biblical myth that interests him, in the way myth was to inform his later poetry, but the possibilities inherent in describing the storm cloud passing over oceans, valleys, and deserts on the way to its destination. The sights on the ground, as the cloud asks God if it should destroy them, occupy a good half of the poem. Here, for example, is a tribe beside the sea:

> *Les enfants, les jeunes filles,*
> *Les guerriers dansaient en rond,*
> *Autour d'un feu sur la grève*
> *Que le vent courbe et relève,*
> *Pareils aux esprits qu'en rêve*
> *On voit tourner sur son front.*

(Children, girls, and warriors were dancing around on the strand by a fire which the wind bows and raises up; they are like spirits in a dream turning about our foreheads.)

The simile gives an odd tone to this evocation, but the passage might be considered somewhat gratuitous. Much the same could be said of the descriptions of Egypt, Babylon, and so forth, except that when we have finished the poem, it becomes clear that these descriptions are its content, that Sodom and Gomorrah merely give the cloud a destination and the poem an end.

Verbal exuberance takes various forms in *Les Orientales*. In the sixth part of "Navarin," nine stanzas are given over to the names and depiction of kinds of ships; almost all of "Grenade" ("Granada") is a list of Spanish cities and their individual beauties. In "Canaris," ostensibly about the hero of the Greek war of independence, a description of warships sinking one another leads to one of flags and their curious detail.

> *L'Autriche a l'aigle étrange, aux ailerons dressés,*
> *Qui, brillant sur la moire,*
> *Vers les deux bouts du monde à la fois menacés*
> *Tourne une tête noire.*
> . . . .
> *L'Angleterre en triomphe impose aux flots amers*
> *Sa splendide oriflamme,*
> *Si riche qu'on prendrait son reflet dans les mers*
> *Pour l'ombre d'une flamme.*

(Austria has the strange eagle with its raised wings, which, glistening on silk, turns its black head toward the two ends of the world, both threatened at once. The bitter waves are subject to triumphant England's splendid oriflamme, one so rich that in the seas its reflection looks like the shadow of a flame.)

Finally, in the last stanza, Canaris appears:

> *Mais le bon Canaris, dont un ardent sillon*
> *Suit la barque hardie,*
> *Sur les vaisseaux qu'il prend, comme son pavillon,*
> *Arbore l'incendie!*

(But good Canaris, whose bold ship is followed by a burning wake, on vessels he captures, for his flag, flies fire.)

The reference is to the fireships used to destroy enemy vessels. The poem is so constructed as to reach a dramatic climax at the end, more so than "Le Feu du ciel," but the lengthy building up to it shows the same fondness for descriptiveness. In fact, the list of twelve flags might seem to impart a certain disproportion to the poem, given how briefly Canaris and his figurative banner appear. The urge to accumulate indications of color, shape, and movement, or merely the variety of nouns designating some general notion like ship, can be perhaps best understood in respect to the descriptive poetry of the later eighteenth century in which periphrasis, within the limits of prescribed vocabulary, had generally obviated any very effective or vivid attempts to paint in words.[1] *Les Orientales* marks the moment in Hugo's career when he felt most strongly the need to assert the pictorial powers of language such as we find them already in Chateaubriand's prose. There was a noticeable shift of emphasis after *Les Orientales*.

Even within the framework of description, however, Hugo, unlike prose writers in general, was not content to rely for his effects on the precise noun, the evocative adjective, or verbs conveying accurate movement or position. We see a constant need to go beyond the barer outlines of statement in his use of metaphoric constructions which do not necessarily render with greater refinement visual or other sense perceptions. In the poem "Mazeppa," a naked man is tied to a wild horse which sets off with him toward the Russian steppe; Hugo embellishes this with a profusion of similes:

> *Un cri part; et soudain voilà que par la plaine*
> *Et l'homme et le cheval, emportés, hors d'haleine,*
> *Sur les sables mouvants,*
> *Seuls, emplissant de bruit un tourbillon de poudre*
> *Pareil au noir nuage où serpente la foudre*
> *Volent avec les vents!*

> *Ils vont. Dans les vallons comme un orage ils passent,*
> *Comme ces ouragans qui dans les monts s'entassent,*
> *Comme un globe de feu;*
> *Puis déjà ne sont plus qu'un point noir dans la brume,*
> *Puis s'effacent dans l'air comme un flocon d'écume*
> *Au vaste océan bleu.*

(A shout bursts forth, and suddenly, there, over the plain, both man and horse, rushing, breathless, on the moving sand, alone, filling a whirlwind of dust with sound, like a black cloud in which lightning twists, fly with the wind. They go on. In valleys they pass like a storm, like tempests stacked up in the mountains, like a ball of fire; then they are only a black point in the mist, then vanish in the air like a fleck of foam in the vast blue ocean.)

The presentation of the ride begins with the concrete indications of the horse and rider speeding away, but very soon similes intervene and begin to accumulate. The comparisons are less intense and less apposite than in the opening lines of "Le Feu du ciel" quoted above. From the standpoint of coherence, "black cloud," "storm," "whirlwind," repeat one another somewhat, while "ball of fire" and "fleck of foam" seem less than well suited to each other, and in an uneasy relation to "black point." These less than perfect lines demonstrate how strongly Hugo felt the need to modulate from the mere lineaments of description into a metaphorical mode far denser than what we would be likely to find in even a very heightened prose description. The rhetoric so characteristic of poetry actually moves *away* from minuteness of depiction to suggest a certain chaotic swirl. Whether this effect of tornadolike movement is at its place here in the poem or provides too early a climax in the description of the rider and horse lost in the elements is a question that a more lengthy study of the poem might bring the reader to answer; it is certainly one worth asking, however, because of the piling up of similes at this point in the narrative.

The tension between the pictorial element in *Les Orientales* and analogical language can be seen with unusual clarity in perhaps the

most familiar anthology piece from the collection, "Les Djinns."
The poem describes, in stanzas of ever-lengthening lines, the arrival
of evil spirits, their passing over, and, in stanzas of decreasing line
length, their disappearance. (We might note here that, while Hugo
was a master of French prosody, he never, with a few exceptions
like the present one, chose especially rare verse forms.) The opening
lines, in their great concision, hint at little that is figurative:

> Murs, ville,   Mer grise
> Et port,   Où brise
> Asile   La brise,
> De mort,   Tout dort.

(Walls, city, and port, death's refuge. Grey sea where the breeze breaks.
All is asleep.)

A simile concludes the second stanza:

> Dans la plaine   Elle brame
> Naît un bruit.   Comme une âme
> C'est l'haleine   Qu'une flamme
> De la nuit.   Toujours suit.

(In the plain a noise is born. It is the breath of night. It bellows like a
soul pursued always by a flame.)

Since Hugo's djinns are more like medieval European demons than
Moslem spirits, the comparison has undeniable appropriateness.
But as the horde approaches, the range of analogies brought in
diversifies considerably: One voice is like a tiny bell; the sound
grows to resemble the great bell of a damned convent; the djinns
crack trees as if they were on fire; the roof of the house bends like
wet grass; the house seems to roll like a leaf, and so forth. Finally
they have passed and sound only like a grasshopper in the distance
or hail on a roof. Then:

> D'étranges syllabes
> Nous viennent encor:
> Ainsi, des arabes
> Quand sonne le cor,
>
> Un chant sur la grève
> Par instants s'élève,
> Et l'enfant qui rêve
> Fait des rêves d'or.

(Strange syllables still come to us; so, when the Arab's horn blows, a song rises fitfully on the strand and sleeping children dream dreams of gold.)

The image is attractive but somewhat irrelevant, especially since in the following stanza *gronder* ("rumble") will be used of the djinns, which hardly suggests a dream-giving chant or song. Almost every stanza of "Les Djinns" contains a comparison or other very overt use of figurative language. They are usually not so evocative as the one just quoted, but they have a tendency to move away from or to suggest other trains of associations than the horde of passing spirits. The initial movement of the poem, to portray djinns in flight, and the working out of the language in individual stanzas result in a certain fitful disparity. Hugo had never before given such rein both to pure description and to analogy, and it is not surprising that the two are as yet unevenly combined in many passages. On the other hand, we do find in places the kind of metaphor characteristic of his mature work in which concrete situations and analogies are closely interwoven. In "Les Têtes du sérail" ("The Heads on the Seraglio"), three Greek soldiers' impaled heads speak; one says of the Sultan:

> *Frères, plaignez Mahmoud! Né dans sa loi barbare,*
> *Des hommes et de Dieu son pouvoir le sépare.*
> *Son aveugle regard ne s'ouvre pas au ciel.*
> *Sa couronne fatale, et toujours chancelante,*
> *Porte à chaque fleuron une tête sanglante;*
> *Et peut-être il n'est pas cruel!*

(Brothers, pity Mahmut. Born into his barbarous law, his power separates him from men and God. His blind eyes do not open to heaven. His fatal crown, forever unsteady, bears on each of its points a bloody head, and perhaps he is not cruel.)

A picture of Istanbul at night, the harem, and its countless mutilated heads gives way here to a vision of the Ottoman ruler's power and weakness, for the revolt of the janissaries is alluded to. The real pikes merge with the ornaments of the crown; the image transforms the actual elements of the scene. The notion of decorative, idle imagery, as opposed to structurally appropriate figurative language, has often been brought to bear on the English Romantics at their expense; in *Les Orientales* we find both kinds of imagery. The more decorative sort tends to prevail, as it probably corresponded to a certain feeling for poetry as evocativeness: However modest the relevance of a metaphor or simile, it is a sign that we are in the domain of the imagination, which is necessarily, after all, the only means of conveying an unknown Orient. With the passage of time and shifting of subject matter, Hugo's figurative language ultimately passed into other, more complex phases.

To go back to the question of unadorned description and the evident discomfort Hugo felt with it, we can turn again to "Mazeppa," where, as we have seen, description is heavily reinforced by similes. Dramatically, or in terms of plot, the situation in the poem remains obscure, for "Mazeppa" is not the whole story of the Polish prince punished for adultery who later became a Cossack hetman, which Byron had already made famous. In fact, Hugo tells nothing of the tale, but merely recounts Mazeppa's wild ride into the Ukraine, relying on the reader's familiarity with Byron to supply the framework. Hugo's poem is divided into two parts, the second of which develops an analogy between Mazeppa's ride and ultimate rise to power with genius bearing its possessor. This bipartite structure, in which the opening section is descriptive and the second part a commentary, is extremely frequent in nineteenth-century verse. However, the kind of poem in which Mazeppa's ride is like this or that can have a rather mechanical quality: We can see how it derives from the lengthy simile and is easily accountable for in rationalistic, rhetorical terms. It is significant that Hugo used it relatively little: He drew away from such a clear-cut way of isolating description from other elements of the poem. There are other analogical effects, much harder to describe within the framework of traditional rhetoric.

The rounding off of a poem by an image which may or may not even be cast in the form of an analogy is quite different from the uses of figurative language we have seen so far. The concluding stanza of "Canaris" quoted above unobtrusively compares hoisting a flag over a ship and setting it on fire; this is not simile-like juxtaposition with connectives such as "thus," "so," and the poem does not break up into two parts, statement and commentary. The analogy is neither logical nor labored, but seems to grow ingeniously out of the preceding material. Elsewhere Hugo attempts, by the expansion of an analogy, to turn it into a very special kind of structural element. In "Le Poète au calife" ("The Poet to the Caliph"), a sultan is described in all his power with Hugo's customary passing metaphors of varying degree of intensity but generally concise. Then at the end:

> *Mais souvent dans ton coeur, radieux Noureddin,*
> *Une triste pensée apparaît, et soudain*
> *Glace ta grandeur taciturne;*
> *Telle en plein jour parfois, sous un soleil de feu,*
> *La lune, astre des morts, blanche au fond d'un ciel bleu*
> *Montre à demi son front nocturne.*

(But often in your heart, radiant Noureddin, a sad thought appears and suddenly chills your silent grandeur; thus sometimes in full day, under a burning sun, the moon, star of the dead, white in the depths of a blue sky, half shows its nighttime face.)

The length of the comparison, the careful choice of details, completely outstrips all previous figurative elements in beauty and unpredictability. In other words, the development and end point of the poem are determined by a gradation of analogies. Again, we see that in an ostensibly descriptive poem the figurative elements of language proliferate and here come to control the structure. There is no visual relation between the sultan's heart and the moon; rather, the image is a luxurious outpouring, whose showiness, by itself, brings about a point of rest.

The same thing can happen, however, on the level of straight description when a statement ceases to have strong narrative value and assumes atmospheric function, which can be, at times, a kind of figurative element. "Les Adieux de l'hôtesse arabe" ("The Farewell of the Arab Hostess") is a generally unmemorable piece, although it comes perhaps closest in its descriptive range to the Arabic poems Hugo quotes prose translations of in his notes to *Les Orientales*: References remain fairly strictly within the framework of Bedouin life and ideas of beauty. It concerns a European lover who is departing, and nothing in its language would seem to bring about a point of repose until an image remote from both the Arab woman and the European comes up:

> *Adieu donc!—Va tout droit. Garde-toi du soleil*
> *Qui dore nos fronts bruns, mais brûle un teint vermeil;*
> *De l'Arabie infranchissable;*
> *De la vieille qui va seule et d'un pas tremblant;*
> *Et de ceux qui le soir, avec un bâton blanc,*
> *Tracent des cercles sur le sable!*

(Farewell, then. Go straight ahead. Beware of the sun, which gilds our dark foreheads, but burns rosy skin, of Arabia which can never be crossed, of the old woman walking alone with a halting step, and of those who in the evening, with a white stick, trace circles on the sand!)

The warning at the end is mysteriously combined with an image of monotony summing up the narrow circle of desert life which the European is doubtless relieved to say good-bye to. It is very difficult to say whether the warning is a threat, whether the desert or its people are the menace. Hugo has gotten a great deal of suggestion with a minimum of means.

Les Orientales concludes with a poem of fading vision as winter life in Paris obliterates the East from the poet's mind. Like "Mazeppa" and "L'Enthousiasme" ("Enthusiasm"), it suggests that imagination is both the method and a theme, now covert, now explicit in the volume. But in technical terms, as we have seen, the nature and limits of description constitute the most important aspect of *Les Orientales*. The relation of description to metaphor and simile constantly comes to our attention in a way it could not with the periphrastic odes, and will concern us far less in Hugo's collections of the 1830's. The reason for this lies partly in the peculiar subject matter of *Les Orientales*, which, consisting of visions, of essentially external notions of exotic places, can only lead to primarily pictorial effects, although it does not escape our attention that Hugo was especially drawn to somewhat gory details in Turkish life. And that brings us to the topic of *l'art pour l'art* and the unique position *Les Orientales* occupies in the history of French Romantic poetry.

After Hugo had claimed that his book was a useless one of pure poetry, the idea of the uselessness of beauty was taken up with great enthusiasm by Théophile Gautier, who was emerging as an important poet of the newest generation. He gave the notion its most famous development in the preface to the novel *Mademoiselle de Maupin* (1835). Gautier's declaration that the most useful part of a house is the sanitary facilities sums up his attitude toward any work of art presented as having a practical purpose. What Gautier does not explicitly say, however, in his long, amusing diatribe is that useless art, pure, disinterested, perfect art, tends toward a certain kind of subject matter, at least in the framework of French Romanticism. We might guess from Gautier's constant allusions to the beaux arts (he himself was briefly a painter) that useless art will have a strong descriptive element. As a matter of fact, his own poetry, to say nothing of that of Leconte de Lisle, another, later, great proponent of useless art, is very rich in the pictorial. Furthermore, the things described are often of the exotic-medieval range, when not artifacts themselves, so that we sense a filiation between the area of subject matter of *Les Orientales* and later manifestations of art for art's sake. The relation is quite clear in the case of Flaubert, for example, on whom *Les Orientales* seems to have had a strong formative action: He loved Hugo and variants of the historical-exotic recur regularly in his work, accompanied by an intransigent insistence on the autonomy of art. In sum, the notion of *l'art pour l'art*, which theoretically should not reject any subject matter, is closely related to certain choices in it.

There is another aspect of these choices as well, which is not to be neglected. Hugo's Turkish world is, as we have noted, characterized by bloody practices like impaling the heads of enemies; in certain works of Gautier and Flaubert a similarly morbid atmosphere prevails. The notion of pure art gradually acquired a distinct connotation of the unhealthy and, ultimately, of perverse immorality. None of this can really be found in *Les Orientales*, but Hugo's taste for picturesque violence is not completely unrelated to the later stages of *l'art pour l'art*. He had by that time ceased to care for this notion, although he claimed to have invented the phrase, but the morbid imaginings found in many of his later works show that by temperament he was not completely alien to the posterity of *Les Orientales*.

II Notre-Dame de Paris

The preface to *Les Orientales* shows Hugo's interest in painting, which his acquaintance with artists of his generation sparked or intensified. His interest in architecture was, however, of apparently earlier origin and longer duration; its effect on his writing is certainly as much in evidence. A taste for medieval architecture was to be expected from any disciple of Chateaubriand, but in the case of Hugo it took a more serious form than usual. His vacations were frequently spent, at least in part, studying Romanesque (he was an early user of the term) and Gothic monuments, and after the publication of *Notre-Dame de Paris* he was appointed to a newly created government committee for their preservation.

It is difficult today to imagine the circumstances surrounding the appearance of *Notre-Dame de Paris* (1831) and its polemic on the beauty and cultural peculiarity of medieval church architecture.[2] We are accustomed to the great cathedrals being treated like museum objects, preserved from the contamination of unsuitable adjoining buildings, and not altered in any way without considerable publicity supported by the views of those considered to have some authority on questions of authenticity. (The cleaning of Notre Dame in the 1960's excited interest far beyond the circle of people having the faintest notion of what state the color of the stones was in at a given time.) In Hugo's day, on the other hand, medieval buildings could be rebuilt, redecorated, sold to anyone, or destroyed. When churches were cleaned, a scraping process was often used which damaged sculpture, whereas simple washing, as is done today, would have sufficed. Worst of all in Hugo's opinion, clerical authorities were free to have precious monuments colored red, yellow, blue, or whatever with plaster-based paints, which seems to have been a great fashion of the day. The process spoiled texture and detail.

Aside from the question of cleaning and maintenance, we must also remember that Paris, when *Notre-Dame de Paris* was published, was much more like the medieval city than it was at the end of the nineteenth century: The grandiose clearing and rebuilding projects of the Second Empire had not yet straightened out the rabbit warren of streets around Notre Dame and other old parts of the city, and restoration of medieval structures was as yet to come. Hugo's novel spoke, therefore, to an audience which knew the city both untouched by proper respect for the cathedral and at the same time more like the medieval one that had seen it grow. Hugo would have perhaps been horrified at both the elegant whiteness and the isolation of the church today, to say nothing of the pious fraud of its excessively loving restoration. In any case, his book was an important gesture in the history of taste and must be thought of in the circumstances of an age when the fate of the cathedrals was a live question.

There is a great deal more, of course, to *Notre-Dame de Paris* than Hugo's concern with architecture, but certain aspects of the novel have assumed their full interest only in the context of Hugo's later work and of the general history of the novel. Let us start with a résumé of the plot, if only to see how imperfectly it represents the work. Here is the description of it given in the *Oxford Companion to French Literature*:

Claude Frollo, archdeacon of Notre Dame, becomes enamoured of Esmeralda, a gypsy dancer, the favorite of the idle Parisian crowds. He employs Quasimodo, the grotesque, hunchback bell-ringer of Notre Dame whom he has succored and befriended, to kidnap her. Esmeralda is rescued by Phoebus de Châteaupers, Captain of the Royal Archers. She falls in love with him, taking him for a hero rather than the loose-living braggart that he is, and agrees to meet him secretly. Frollo follows her to the rendez-vous, stabs Phoebus before her eyes, and escapes, leaving her to be arrested and sentenced to death for his crime. Quasimodo, whom one casual act of kindness has made her slave, snatches her from the scaffold itself and brings her secretly to sanctuary in the Cathedral. Frollo so engineers matters that the band of gypsies, beggars, and malefactors to whom Esmeralda belongs learn of her hiding place and determine to rescue her. They make a midnight attack upon the Cathedral (one of the most dramatic scenes of the book) and are repulsed by Quasimodo, single-handed. Meantime Frollo, in disguise, has persuaded Esmeralda to fly with him. Suddenly she recognizes him and chooses to be denounced to the authorities rather than yield to his threats. Frollo, enraged, goes off to find the officers of the guard, leaving Esmeralda in charge of a half-mad woman whose daughter had been kidnapped by gypsies some years previously. Suddenly the woman sees by an amulet the girl is wearing that Esmeralda is her daughter. At this moment the archers arrive. After almost superhuman efforts they wrest Esmeralda from her mother, leaving the old woman dying on the pavement. From one of the towers of Notre Dame Quasimodo, in despair, sees Esmeralda's body swinging to and fro on the gallows. He turns and discovers Frollo gloating over the same scene. With one movement he dashes him from the balustrade to the cobblestones far below. One day, in the vault where criminals' corpses are flung, Quasimodo's skeleton is found beside that of Esmeralda.

This is at once very accurate and yet unrevealing of certain essential qualities of the novel, and first of all of the pacing of the story, the effects of heightening created by the way elements of it are introduced.

The novel opens on a festive day in Paris in January, 1482 (chronology is carefully indicated in the book, and the action divided among some twelve days spread over six months: Hugo's minute planning is evident). About a fifth of the entire length is taken up with this day's events, which include a mystery play and the peculiar celebration known as the *fête des fous*. Everything is seen through the eyes of a secondary character, Pierre Gringoire, who does not realize, any more clearly than the reader may at first, the feelings Frollo has for Esmeralda or that he attempts to abduct her. This effect of obscurity is essential to Hugo's design, for while elements of the plot are present, they must not begin to tighten in a causal chain until the thematics of the novel have emerged. The following books continue the exposition of medieval life with chapters on the shape of Paris and the cathedral, but Gringoire's narrative point of view is dropped, being no longer relevant. The purpose of postponing the descriptions of the city as seen from Notre Dame as well as of the church itself is to tie them more closely to the story of Quasimodo's origins, which follows, and to the scenes involving Frollo's hermetic interpretation of the sculpture of the façade and the exposition of his philosophical concerns. We focus first on the church as a work of art; then Hugo begins to suggest the grotesque and sinister spirit informing the edifice, which is personified in Frollo and Quasimodo. The plan of the first half of the novel is to move us from a festive mood to a somber one, from crowds on the ground to the two odd creatures climbing about the recesses of Notre Dame.

This kind of fictional structure, in which a long, carefully planned out introductory section provides the necessary characters, situations, and motives for what will follow was to occur in certain Balzac novels, but Balzac had not yet devised it at the time of *Notre-Dame de Paris*. (There is no question but that Balzac's first novel signed with his own name, *Les Chouans*, and those immediately following it are vastly inferior to Hugo's novel in respect to design.) It is not a familiar modern form of fiction, and the present-day reader may be disconcerted at the amount of material brought in before he discerns the forward momentum of plot. It is, on the other hand, a perfectly viable shape for a novel in which thematic material— here, the character of Notre Dame and medieval Paris—determines the way the plot will move. Our expectations of plot movement are, in a sense, arbitrary, since that is only one aspect of a novel's form, and sometimes a subordinate one.

The crucial section of *Notre-Dame de Paris* which lies between the long exposition and Frollo's attempt to murder Phoebus gives us the central symbol of the novel as well as some suggestive glosses on it. We know from an earlier chapter, typical in the seemingly casual way it has been introduced, that the archdeacon believes in alchemy above astrology, medicine, and the other arts, and that he interprets the sculptures of Notre Dame in an alchemical sense. Now Jehan, Frollo's younger brother, comes to see him and in the chapter entitled "'ANATKH" two things are impressed upon us. The first is the spider's web in the window, resembling the rose window of Notre Dame, and, by extension, medieval thought; the second is Frollo's identification of gold with the sun, a subject on which he meditates and whose relation with the web in the window starts to become overt. Although Hugo will spell out his symbolic meanings to a considerable extent, their richness and anchorage in reality is remarkable and prevents their seeming quickly exhausted or contrived. But the meaning of *anangke* ("fate") which Frollo writes upon the wall, and its relevance to the spider and the sun is withheld until the following chapter where the representative of secular law, Charmolue, comes to see the archdeacon about trying Esmeralda for practice of magic. The passage must be quoted rather fully:

> Don Claude, lost in his own thought, did not hear him. Charmolue, following the direction of his gaze saw that it was fixed mechanically upon the large spider web which covered the window. At this instant a rash fly, in search of the March sun, plunged headlong into the trap and was caught in it. At the vibration of its web the huge spider made a sudden sally from its central cell, and with one bound fell upon the fly, which it doubled up with its front antennae, while its hideous proboscis dug out the head. "Poor fly!" said the king's proxy to the Ecclesiastical Court; and he raised his hand to save it. The archdeacon, with a start, held back his arm with convulsive force.
> "Master Jacques," he cried, "do not interfere with the work of Fate!"

That Frollo is a heretic and damned we have already suspected; here he openly denies the possibility of salvation. But there is more: Hugo is not simply using fate in the general, somewhat convenient way that many French Romantics did. It has a greater application in the case of Frollo than merely his passion for Esmeralda:

> "Oh yes," added the priest, in a voice which seemed to come from his very entrails, "this is a universal symbol. The insect flies about, is happy, is young; it seeks the spring sun, the fresh air, freedom; oh, yes, but it runs against the fatal web; the spider appears—the hideous spider! poor dancing-girl! poor predestined fly! Master Jacques, do not interfere! it is the hand of Fate! Alas! Claude, you are the spider. Claude, you are the fly as well! You flew abroad in search of learning, light, the sun; your only desire was

to gain the pure air, the broad light of eternal truth; but in your haste to reach the dazzling window which opens into the other world—the world of intellect, light, and learning—blind fly! senseless doctor! you failed to see that subtle spider's web woven by Fate between the light and you; you plunged headlong into it, wretched fool! and now you struggle in its meshes, with bruised head and broken wings, in the iron grasp of destiny. Master Jacques, Master Jacques, let the spider do its work!"

Frollo's learning cannot pierce the "crystal wall harder than iron which separates all philosophy from truth." Now we see the relation between the spider and the cathedral, the web and the rose window. As has been made clear in the comments on church architectural ornaments as a kind of book, a summa of arcane knowledge, Notre Dame itself represents the philosophy which imprisons the archdeacon. The cathedral and the culture which produced it are in the grips of a sinister force, promising but withholding truth. The beautiful rose window is actually the spider web which will destroy those who approach it seeking life and light.

There is another link in the symbolism of the novel between Frollo's obsession with Esmeralda and his search for truth. In the monologue overheard by Jehan, the archdeacon ponders the means to extract gold from fire and light:

Magistri declares that there are certain feminine names possessing so sweet and mysterious a spell that it is enough to pronounce them during the operation. Let us read what Manu says under this head: "Where women are reverenced, the divinities rejoice; where they are scorned, it is vain to pray to God. A woman's mouth is ever pure; it is like running water, it is like a sunbeam."

In other words, Frollo's reckless passion for the gypsy dancer is actually a further temptation to discover the mendacious truth of alchemy. Hugo has tightly woven together all the aspects of Frollo's personality so that his jealous murder attempt on Phoebus ("the sun"), Esmeralda's lover, seems to stem in part from his frustration as a seeker of wisdom. The means and decision to kill Phoebus follow directly on his outbursts in the presence of Charmolue. It is an old commonplace that Hugo's characters are thin and simplistic. Such a judgment has its obvious element of truth, but is inadequate for Frollo. The philosophical crisis which he reaches is remarkably built up and is inseparable from the whole idea of the cathedral as a misleading book of wisdom, which dominates the work.

One question arises in connection with the theme of fate. As we have seen, it is complexly worked out. Can we say, however, that it corresponds to any deep-rooted preoccupation on Hugo's part? Fate is a handy theme in narrative; Hugo's contemporaries such as Mérimée or Vigny did not fail to exploit it. One might be tempted to dismiss it as a convenient resounding term. On the other hand, in Hugo's philosophical poetry of the late 1850's the idea of fate takes its place in a reasonably elaborate scheme of thought. For the psychoanalytically oriented Baudouin, fate and the spider represent evil female sexuality, *la mère terrible*, who will in one form or another haunt Hugo's imagination;[3] psychoanalytic criticism, however, does not bother to ask what an author's themes and symbols could have meant for him. Hugo states in his first preface to the novel that the whole book grew out of his meditation on finding the word *anangke* scratched on a wall in Notre Dame. Whether he really found this or not is unimportant; I think, however, that we should take him fairly literally in one sense. The symbol, that is, medieval architecture, came first; its sense then emerged for Hugo. This would seem to be the imaginative process characteristic of his work, as seen in its entire evolution. He found his symbols, and the latent patterns of his thought, his philosophy of good and evil, took form around them. In *Notre-Dame de Paris* the theme of fate has as yet no general philosophical dimension, but is tied to a poetic vision of the Middle Ages. Only later will it take on a broader meaning.

The imagery of the spider, web, sun, and window recurs in *Notre-Dame de Paris* as the plot gathers momentum and plunges toward its conclusion.[4] Now we may better see the design of the novel: A tremendous amount of expository material, even when it only serves, as it doubtless does at times, to create atmosphere, is necessary to lead up to the symbolic identification of the cathedral, fate, alchemy, and Frollo's desire for Esmeralda. The setting of the novel in the fifteenth century does not permit Hugo to make assumptions about the reactions of the reader; the latter must be thoroughly familiar with Hugo's conception of medieval life—stylized and demonic as it obviously is—in order to accept Frollo's spiritual crisis from which the tighter section of the plot derives. At the same time, however, Hugo has, through his scenes of medieval life, so carefully prepared the second half of the novel that we are not aware of any inartistic break in continuity or abrupt change of pace in narration. To take a small but important example, Quasimodo's trial for disturbance of the peace in the first half of the novel prepares us for the picture of the courts and justice we find later. This is but one of countless ways in which units of the narrative are linked together. It would take an immensely elaborate diagram to show them all.

Narrative continuity in *Notre-Dame de Paris* is also a function of style, and here again we may favorably compare Hugo's work with certain aspects of Balzac's fiction, even though the latter was unquestionably the greater novelist. Both writers comment on their characters and plots, but Hugo's verbal medium is so polished in its rhythms, his interventions so much in the tone of his characters' odd turns of mind, that we have little feeling of digressions breaking or hindering the movement of the work. Proust, attempting to explain a similar difference between Balzac and Flaubert, contrasted "all the elements of a style which is still to come . . . undigested and untransformed" in *La Comédie humaine* (*The Human Comedy*) with Flaubert's "one unanimous substance, . . . vast, unvarying polished surfaces." Like Flaubert, who so greatly admired his work, Hugo knew how to weld together description, dialogue, summary narration and other components of fiction into a whole through his sense of congruity of every word and sentence pattern. Hugo's style is often said to derive from Chateaubriand's, but actually they share only a taste for long sentences with careful rhythmic articulations. Hugo's descriptive writing is not lush or nostalgic like the older writer's, and his fondness for epigrammatic statements, often in an antithetical form, is recognizably his own. Furthermore, in *Notre-Dame de Paris* he was obliged, especially for the purposes of dialogue, to create a diction which would be neither tediously archaic nor unduly anachronistic. Only a detailed linguistic study of the work would show precisely how he achieved this; the problem is an intricate, absorbing one.

Notre-Dame de Paris was not the only piece of fiction Hugo wrote between *Bug-Jargal* and his late novels. *Le Dernier Jour d'un condamné* (1829) is the very antithesis of the highly aesthetic preoccupations we have examined in this chapter; it is a short, *engagé* study of prison life, written to combat capital punishment. The use of argot in it is unusual at so early a date in the nineteenth-century novel, but its structure is somewhat loose, so that it is not technically a very important work. However, its contemporaneity with *Les*

Orientales constitutes a striking example of Hugo's simultaneous yet diverging literary interests. And the earlier ones among the plays, to which we shall turn now, coincide also with Hugo's working out new problems in lyric and fiction. A strictly chronological approach to his work would show a baffling interweaving of various projects and concerns.

CHAPTER 3

Plays through Les Burgraves

I *Generalities*

H UGO'S urge to write plays began early and lasted late—later than the period covered in this chapter. It began and ended with plays which were never acted, though for different reasons. His first efforts show considerable versatility; they include *Irtamène* (1816), a tragedy; *AQCHEB* ("A quelque chose hasard est bon" [Chance is Good for Something]), a *vaudeville*, that is, a comedy with songs; and *Inez de Castro* (1818), a *mélodrame*, which was a sensational drama with music. As is obvious, he tried genres ranging from the subliterary up through the Neoclassical tragedy. His experiment in the last form, *Irtamène*, is most worthy of note: It is an irregular tragedy (the unities of time and place are not observed; the ending is happy), but the style is an astonishingly perfect exercise in the manner of Racine. All his later remarks on the shortcomings of Neoclassical tragedy were not the carpings of one who had never known the manner; Hugo, as in his *Odes*, had thoroughly absorbed a Neoclassical poetic style before rejecting it.

For the middle period of his dramatic opus, from *Cromwell* (1827) to *Les Burgraves* (1843), we had best summarize certain external facts about Hugo's theatrical career before looking at any plays in detail, for the theater had an exceptional importance in his *oeuvre* during these years: It caught the attention of the public as no other genre could so quickly, and it was far more remunerative than "pure," "useless" poetry.

Since the high point of Neoclassical poetry had been in the genre of tragedy, it was evident that the new poetry of the nineteenth century would have to prove itself in the theater so that the new aesthetic not be judged lacking. Hugo wrote *Cromwell* in 1826–27, as the *Odes et Ballades* (1826) were being readied for another edition. For reasons that are not clear, *Cromwell* turned out to be at least three times as long as a conventional verse play and was not performed, despite the fact that audiences of the day were accustomed to Wagnerian-length evenings at the theater. Hugo made up for the lack of performance by writing a long preface (1827) which is one of the few important statements of literary principles in the French Romantic movement and in his career. In place of *Cromwell* he prepared a really playable work, *Marion de Lorme*, in 1829. This was to have been the first verse play of the French Romantic movement to reach the stage. Unfortunately, the royal censor deemed it offensive to Charles X that Louis XIII be an unsympathetic character in a play. (Since Hugo's other opinions always changed in function of artistic concerns, his views on the legitimate monarchy declined accordingly.) Again, Hugo made up for an irritating situation: He wrote *Hernani* with his usual rapidity; it was performed (1830) at the Comédie Française, the most conservative of theaters, caused a sensation partly through careful publicity stunts, and left Hugo, as usual, far ahead of his contemporaries in his reputation for brilliance and daring. From this point on, the theater was to count for a good deal, during a few years at least, in Hugo's income and preoccupations. After *Le Roi s'amuse* (1832), which ran into difficulties this time with Louis Philippe's censors, he ceased, perhaps through financial concerns, to maintain that verse was the proper vehicle of Romantic drama: *Lucrèce Borgia* (1833) and *Marie Tudor* (1833) are prose plays, as is *Angelo* (1835).

A certain distaste for the actual conditions of stage productions came over Hugo after *Angelo*, thanks to a long series of problems with actors and managements. However, he suddenly received a remarkable kind of encouragement: Through the good offices of the Duchesse d'Orléans, the wife of the heir to the throne, a German princess who arrived in France loving French literature and above all Hugo, he was offered a new theater and a say in how it was to be run. For the Théâtre de la Renaissance he wrote *Ruy Blas* (1838). Another play, *Les Jumeaux*, was never finished. Finally, his last play performed, *Les Burgraves*, was a failure in 1843. By this time, however, Hugo was a member of the Academy, well connected at court, and in considerably less need of the financial and moral support of the theater, which he thereupon abandoned. His later dramatic works, which he made no effort to have performed, belong to another phase of his career as a poet.

The background of Hugo's plays has sometimes been analyzed in terms of the various genres, *mélodrame, drame bourgeois*, historical play, and so forth, which enjoyed favor in the early nineteenth century. Certainly there is no question that the melodramatic, which characterized many of these plays—the *mélodrame* itself being specifically a play with music—contributed toward the formation of Hugo's taste in plot structures and choice of characters. However, Hugo was primarily a poet, and we must not forget that he wrote primarily poetic drama, which implies more complex choices in style than any of the ephemeral and subliterary works of the Romantic period. Much the same objection must also be made to any attempt to treat Hugo's theatrical production solely in terms of dramaturgy, the art of constructing an action for illusory characters. There is much of interest in this approach, but again Hugo was predominantly a writer of poetic plays, a fact we must not lose sight of. The interplay between these divergent aspects of his dramas will necessarily be a recurrent topic as we look at some of the more interesting of them.

II Cromwell *and its Preface*

Hugo chose a historical subject, as he would consistently later, for *Cromwell*, the first of his published verse dramas, and we should see the significance of this against the background of German drama, particularly that of Schiller. We must remember that Hugo did not compete with obscure literary figures, that the most famous dramatists outside the French Neoclassical tradition, Shakespeare, Schiller, and the Spaniards, were his rivals. The modern German drama was the closest in time and probably the most relevant for directing Hugo's attention to sixteenth- and seventeenth-century subjects. In any case, Hugo, as usual, did not depict any real event in *Cromwell*, but based his plot on an element of reality, the possibility that the Protector would have been declared King of England. (There are certain curious similarities with *Julius Caesar*.)

The plot of this immense play is in many ways quite simple. In Act I ("The Conspirators"—Hugo began his habit of entitling his acts like chapters), Royalists meet with fervent Roundheads to plan the assassination of Cromwell, for fear he will accept Parliament's scheme to elevate him to the throne. Among them are Carr, a fanatic Puritan, and Rochester, whom Hugo, by some confusion perhaps, identified with the Restoration poet, and Richard, Cromwell's own son. Act II ("The Spies") centers on Cromwell, who receives ambassadors, gets wind of the plot, and meets Rochester disguised as his new chaplain. Carr having betrayed them, the Cavalier conspirators decide to murder Cromwell that very night. Cromwell's four jesters and the predictions of Manassé, the Jewish usurer-cum-astrologer-cum-necromancer, occupy the third act until, at the end, Rochester is made to drink the sleeping potion intended for the Protector. Cromwell himself serves as palace guard in Act IV ("The Sentinel") and summons men-in-arms as the Royalists discover the sleeping man they would kill is actually Rochester. Act V ("The Workers") shows the preparations for Cromwell's crowning, his refusal of the scepter, and the general pardon he grants the conspirators.

As is clear from this résumé, Cromwell knows for three acts about the plot against him and only the details of foiling the Royalists, very simple details at that, are in question. From the standpoint of character development, Cromwell's change of heart about the kingship, prompted by Manassé's warnings about his star, constitutes the sole psychological problem of the drama. What then takes up these five long acts? The answer is simply elaborate appearances of minor characters such as John Milton and extraordinary dialogues and speeches. From the very beginning, as Cavaliers and Puritans make suspicious contact with each other, Hugo's delight in representing styles of speech is evident. The Roundheads use biblical images and references, the Royalists a neutral diction except for the Frenchified Rochester who speaks with Neoclassical elegances. As the play progresses, the verbal brilliance increases: Act III, in which little happens in any ordinary sense, is especially remarkable. The jesters sing crazy songs on the Shakespearean model; Milton and Rochester discuss poetry. The latter declares his love for Cromwell's daughter in the style of the French *précieux*:

> *Ce papier de mon coeur vous fera le tableau,*
> *Il eût été détruit par la flamme ou par l'eau,*
> *Si mon feu n'eût séché mes pleurs, et si, Madame,*
> *Mes larmes à leur tour n'eussent éteint ma flamme!*
> *Prenez, lisez, jugez de mon amour ardent!*

(This paper will depict for you my heart; it would have been destroyed by fire or water if my love's flame had not dried my tears, and if, Madame, in turn, my tears had not put out my flame. Take it, read, judge of my burning love.)

Cromwell, like the other Puritans, thinks constantly in biblical archetypes; when he is asked the best way of putting to death dis-

senters, referred to in the Roundhead periphrasis as those who
mispronounce Shibboleth (see Judges 12:4–6), he replies:

> La question est grave et veut être murie.
> Prononcer Siboleth, c'est une idolâtrie.
> Crime digne de mort, dont sourit Belzébuth.
> Mais tout supplice doit avoir un double but,
> Que pour le patient l'humanité réclame;
> En châtiant son corps, il faut sauver son âme.
> Or quel est le meilleur de la corde ou du feu
> Pour réconcilier un pécheur avec Dieu?
> Le feu le purifie . . .
>   (Rochester, à part : Et la corde l'étrangle.)
> Daniel s'épura dans le brûlant triangle.
> Mais la potence a bien son avantage aussi;
> La croix fut un gibet.

(The question is serious and should be thought on. Pronouncing "Sib-
boleth" is idolatry, a crime deserving death, making Beelzebub smile. But
every torture should have a double aim, which simple humanity requires
for the victim; by punishing his body, we must save his soul. Now which is
better, the rope or the fire, to reconcile a sinner with God? Fire purifies . . .
[Rochester, aside: And the rope strangles.] Daniel cleansed himself in the
burning triangle. But the gallows certainly have their advantage as well;
the cross was a gibbet.)

Hugo brilliantly puts together such speeches in which biblical
allusion, theology, and symbolic interpretations form so elaborate
a tissue as to constitute a genuine mode of thought. Later, in Act
IV, when Cromwell shouts for the guards, the first words that
spring automatically to his lips are *Hors des tentes, Jacob! Israël,
hors des tentes!* His mind is completely allegorical in its processes
and his speech is almost a kind of code. The workmen who plot to
kill him at the beginning of Act V reply to the objection that stabbing
is not a suitable death for Cromwell:

> Le sabre de Judith
> Est frère des couteaux qui vont frapper sa tête.
> Dans l'arsenal du ciel leur place est déjà prête.

(Judith's saber is the brother of the knives which will strike his head;
in heaven's arsenal their place is prepared.)

This devious, roundabout way of transforming reality by constantly
glossing it with scriptural archetypes is, in the case of Carr, who

refuses the proffered amnesty at the end of the play, an expression of complete inability to see concrete situations, so great is his fanaticism. When he casts anathema on Cromwell, his mind wanders, full of the imagery of the prophets, from biblical figure to figure:

> *Mais Dieu fait toujours naître, et c'est l'effroi de l'âme,*
> *Le malheur du bonheur, la cendre de la flamme,*
> *Or Isboseth tomba, tel qu'un fruit avorté,*
> *Tel qu'un bruit sans écho par le vent emporté.*

(But God always causes, and that is the soul's terror, sorrow to be born from happiness, ashes from flame. Now Ishbosheth fell, like a blasted fruit, like a sound carried away without an echo by the wind.)

Hugo has perfectly caught a special cast of mind in his Puritans: Their energy is generated by the feeling of providential design in all they do, and their speech betrays their view of reality as doubled by ever-present symbolic meanings. Cromwell explains his refusal of the crown in terms of the complexity of God's preestablished pattern for the world:

> *On croirait que ce Dieu, terrible aux Philistins,*
> *A comme un ouvrier composé nos destins;*
> *Que son bras, sur un axe indestructible aux âges,*
> *De ce vaste édifice a scellé les rouages,*
> *Oeuvre mystérieuse, et dont ses longs efforts*
> *Pour des siècles peut-être ont monté les ressorts.*
> *Ainsi tout va. La roue, à la roue enchaînée,*
> *Mord de sa dent de fer la machine entraînée;*
> *Les massifs balanciers, les antennes, les poids,*
> *Labyrinthe vivant, se meuvent à la fois;*
> *L'effrayante machine accomplit sans relâche*
> *Sa marche inexorable et sa puissante tâche;*
> *Et des peuples entiers, pris dans ses mille bras,*
> *Disparaîtraient broyés, s'ils ne se rangeaient pas.*
> *Et j'entraverais Dieu, dont la loi salutaire*
> *Nous fait un sort à part dans le sort de la terre!*
> *J'irais du peuple élu foulant le droit ancien,*
> *Mettre mon intérêt à la place du sien!*
> *Pilote, j'ouvrirais la voile aux vents contraires!*

(It seems as if this God, terrible for the Philistines, has put together our destinies like a workman, that his arm sealed the machinery of this vast edifice on an axis which the ages cannot destroy—a mysterious creation, whose springs his long toil has wound up for centuries. So all moves. The wheel bound to the wheel bites with its iron tooth the running machine. The huge pendulums, antennas, weights, a living labyrinth, move all at once. The frightening machine accomplishes without ceasing its task as it moves inexorably forward. And entire peoples, caught in its thousand arms, would disappear and be crushed, if they did not leap aside. And you want me to hold back God, whose salutary law has made for us a fate apart in the fate of the earth. And you want me to trample the ancient right of the people, place my interests before theirs! I, the steersman, should open the sail to unfavorable winds!)

The Protector's imagery is notable for its not, for once, being biblical: This picture of a mechanism is designed to bring to the reader's mind the idea of a sinister machine, which is a commentary on Cromwell's God. (Note, however, the marvelous change in imagery at the end of the quotation from tight, bound-in, metallic things to open sea spaces: The abrupt shift is typical of Hugo's great command of style.) The same mechanical image will, in fact, recur in later plays of Hugo's, designating the plot itself; it is an early occurrence in his work of the kind of inhuman, in this case metallic, demonic symbol which was later to occupy his imagination considerably.

Quite aside from all questions of "playableness," *Cromwell* is one of Hugo's most remarkable pieces of dramatic poetry. The diffuseness of the work, its superabundance of interesting but loosely attached scenes, in no way harms the power of characterization we feel in speech after speech, which comes from the distinctive linguistic and literary grounding of Puritan habits of thought. Hugo was dealing primarily with characters whose lives were directed by a book filled with poetry; they lend themselves perfectly to verse drama. The whole problem of finding a style for a character from another age and another country did not arise with *Cromwell*, for Hugo already knew the Bible thoroughly. The task of recreation of the archetypal, allegorical approach to reality is, of course, another matter, and therein lies Hugo's accomplishment as a dramatist and not simply as a poet. Although Hugo's knowledge of writing for stage production expanded greatly after *Cromwell*, he did not by any means surpass this play when it came to rendering his characters' manner of thinking and feeling. In fact, one criticism usually made of Hugo's plays—that the characters are merely shallow figures caught up in a plot—is not especially applicable to

Cromwell, where the individual speeches have greater impact than the plot line.

Cromwell was and has remained completely overshadowed by the lengthy preface Hugo wrote for it, which attempted to justify certain innovations in the theater. This preface is almost as interesting for what Hugo does not say or does not emphasize as it is for his best-known pronouncements. A long introduction, derived from Chateaubriand, divides literature into three stages, that of lyric poetry, epic, and the *drame*. The latter term distinguishes the genre Hugo is arguing in favor of from Neoclassical tragedy, and, inevitably, Shakespeare is put forth as the great model. The drama (we shall simply transpose the special term into English) is characteristic of Christian culture and the dualism of body and spirit which marks it; only through it can modern man express himself adequately. Hugo appeals to nature and truth to demonstrate the validity of this. He does not point out, however, that his argument by nature and truth is precisely the same neo-Aristotelian one which was used in the seventeenth century to affirm or deny the unities of time and place as well as the elusive thing called decorum. The preface to *Cromwell* is, in fact, aimed at a reader to whom Neoclassical lines of argument are completely natural. Hugo defends verse, for example, as being merely a more concentrated form of truth and of nature and reality. Such fundamental questions as why a play should be divided into five acts are not even touched on. In short, Hugo is arguing for a form of play which is different in detail from Neoclassical tragedy, though not radically different in the whole conception of theater it presupposes. Therefore we find many allusions to Molière and polemics over Corneille, Hugo taking a position in favor of relaxed versification and straightforward diction.

The most famous part of the preface concerns "the grotesque." As a development of his remarks on the dualism of spirit and matter in modern, that is, Christian times, Hugo uses this term as the antithesis of the sublime and as the necessary complement to it. Grotesque, as a term, was originally a designation for the grimacing figures, such as *mascheroni*, found in Roman and Renaissance decorative art; by it Hugo suggests something that borders on the comic but is not completely identifiable with it. Lowness of style, in the Neoclassical hierarchy of styles, which corresponds to a social one, comes closest perhaps to being a synonym for Hugo's grotesque.

(Again we notice how imbued Hugo is with Neoclassical modes of thought, even though he deliberately uses a new terminology.) The low style, like the grotesque, embraces both the coarser levels of comedy or farce and satire, the latter shading off into vituperation devoid of humorous intent. In practice, Hugo seems, by his notion of joining the sublime and the grotesque, to advocate both a mingling of tones among scenes of a play and within the portrayal of a single character. *Cromwell* fits this scheme which Hugo's later plays will not always do or only do to a limited extent. It is often forgotten that any writer tries to renew himself, to obtain effects he has hitherto not imagined, and that the preface to *Cromwell* cannot be taken as an exact account of works which Hugo had not yet even conceived of. The habit of considering it as an absolute statement of what the Romantic drama was to consist of is a somewhat careless one.

III   Marion de Lorme

After *Cromwell* Hugo needed, in order to fulfill his own and his admirers' expectations, a really playable work; the result was *Marion de Lorme*, again a seventeenth-century subject with certain stylistic implications, though this time a French one. Again, the grounding of the play in historical reality has only a very general truth; the plot is entirely invented.

The subtitle of the play is "Un Duel sous Richelieu" ("A Duel under Richelieu") and Richelieu's edict punishing dueling by death forms the "inexorable machine" behind the play's action. The courtesan Marion de Lorme, incognito, has taken refuge in Blois with a lover of mysterious origins, Didier, who, by chance, saves her former lover, Saverny, from an attack by thugs. In a drinking scene Didier and Saverny fight a duel in defiance of Richelieu's proclamation; the former is arrested, the latter presumed dead. At Saverny's uncle's château, Didier, who has escaped from prison (a very gratuitous and unmotivated plot element), arrives with Marion and a troupe of strolling players. Didier learns with disgust of Marion's true identity, and when a magistrate examines them, he surrenders, as does Saverny, who has been present in disguise. Marion's attempt, in Act IV, to gain clemency from Louis XIII succeeds, only to be countermanded in the fifth act, when Didier, having forgiven Marion for a last act of prostitution in her effort to save him, and Saverny are executed in Richelieu's satisfied presence.

There is a bifurcation in the forces which carry along the play, one which recurs in various forms later in Hugo's dramas and which is rather puzzling to analyze according to the Neoclassical theory of dramatic action. The play is about both a duel under Richelieu and a peculiar central character called Didier, who seems not to share the privileged nobility's outrage at the restraint put by the cardinal-minister on their fighting habits. It is not at all clear, as his character has been presented, why he fights a duel in the first place; the vagueness of his escape from prison compounds this uncertainty about the why and how of the play between the second and third acts. Didier appears at first as a "humorous" character, in the old sense of someone suffering from an excess of one of the body's emotive secretions; he is splenetic and misanthropic:

> *Si bien que me voici, jeune encore et pourtant*
> *Vieux, et du monde las comme on l'est en sortant;*
> *Ne me heurtant à rien où je ne me déchire;*
> *Trouvant le monde mal, mais trouvant l'homme pire.*

(So here I am, young and yet old, tired of the world as if I were leaving it, torn by whatever I brush against, finding the world bad and mankind worse.)

Molière's Alceste tends to come to mind, for his isolation as well as for his devotion to a single lady. The analogy is further suggested by the air of seventeenth-century *galant* language in the speech of Marion and Saverny. It is quite clear that Hugo's taste for Baroque writers and for Molière inspired certain stylistic contrasts in *Marion de Lorme* and tended to root the play in literary-linguistic reality. Didier, foreseeing his death, speaks in the words of the Louis XIII writers Gautier was to call grotesque for their graveyard imagery:

> *Que le bec du vautour déchire mon étoffe,*
> *Ou que le ver la ronge, ainsi qu'il fait d'un roi,*
> *C'est l'affaire du corps: mais que m'importe, à moi:*
> *Lorsque la lourde tombe a clos notre paupière,*
> *L'âme lève du doigt le couvercle de pierre,*
> *Et s'envole . . .*

(Whether the vulture's beak tears my flesh or the worm gnaws it, just like a king's, it is the body's business, and what difference does it make to me? When the heavy tomb has closed our eyelids, the soul raises the stone cover with its finger and takes flight.)

Didier, in short, sounds like a Baroque poet among salon ones. This aspect of playing with historical poetic styles can be felt strongly in the drinking scene in the second act, and even more so when, in the third, the actors are invited to deliver speeches from plays ranging from Garnier to Corneille. Arbitrariness in the action is somewhat covered up by Hugo's attempt to blend stylistic effects into a medley suggestive of the early seventeenth century.

There are certain aspects of the play, however, which cannot be assimilated to historical poetic styles. Louis XIII, like Cromwell, is an unfathomable, quirky character, and his speeches try to render this with abrupt shifts in mood:

> Cardinal au dehors, cardinal au dedans,
> Le roi jamais!—Il mord l'Autriche à belles dents . . .
> Que sais-je? . . . Il est partout comme l'âme du roi,
> Emplissant mon royaume, et ma famille, et moi!
> Ah! je suis bien à plaindre!
> (Allant à la fenêtre) Et toujours de la pluie!

(The cardinal outside, inside, the king never. He bites into Austria ferociously . . . More, he is everywhere like the king's soul, filling my kingdom, my family, and me. Ah! my lot is wretched. [Going to the window] And it's still raining.)

Louis could not be *galant* like the other characters, nor would Baroque imagery of death fit him as it does Didier. He stands out as the grotesque figure in the play, following Hugo's conception of the term. The fact that Louis appears only in the fourth act, that he is not simply one character among the others, gives a certain imbalance to the stylistic working out of the play, an imbalance we also feel in the plot structure: Since Didier has discovered Marion's identity and will have nothing more to do with her, her attempt to obtain clemency for him from the King is a diversion which will not affect their relations.

Hugo's attempts to enhance Didier's role, to make of him more than merely an odd, gloomy figure among the others leads to emphasis here and there on his sense of fate and the uniqueness of his relationship with Marion; Didier is commonly considered the first example of a Byronic Romantic hero in Hugo's work, a hero of a kind to be found abundantly in lesser writers of the period. Yet his language is only intermittently anachronistic; much of it remains in the early seventeenth-century vein of death poetry, one of the most interesting aspects of the play. With *Hernani*, Hugo realized, for better or for worse, a far more exemplary Romantic hero, who does not remind us in any way of a particular historical context.

IV   Hernani

The plot of *Hernani* is far more complicated than that of Hugo's previous plays, and a résumé will necessarily fail, as in the case of *Notre-Dame de Paris*, to suggest anything like the involution of its details. At the beginning, the duenna of a noble Spanish girl, Doña Sol, hides Don Carlos, the King of Spain, when Doña Sol receives her aspiring lover, Hernani, whose father, though noble, had perished by royal order. Doña Sol's fiancé and uncle, Don Ruy Gomez de Silva, enters. The latter is told the King has come to discuss his elevation to Holy Roman Emperor. (We are in 1519, and the King is the future Charles V, but the events and characters have no historical grounding whatsoever.) A troubadour scene follows, in which Hernani permits the King, who has come to serenade and abduct Doña Sol, to go scot free (a question of honor). In the third act, Doña Sol's wedding to Don Ruy Gomez is interrupted by the arrival of Hernani (spared, as a guest, by the *pundonor*), and then by that of the King, who carries off Doña Sol. Act IV takes place in Aachen where, simultaneously, Don Carlos is elected Emperor, and conspirators, among them Hernani and Don Ruy Gomez, plot to kill him. He grants a general pardon, and Hernani is revealed to be not a bandit, but a grandee of Spain. At the time when Don Carlos had carried off Doña Sol, Hernani and Don Ruy Gomez had agreed that after the former killed the King, the latter would have the right to demand Hernani's suicide. This is what happens in the final act, even though, of course, the King has not been killed.

The unexpected points of honor invoked and the sudden reversals of attitude on the part of the characters unquestionably contributed to the public reaction to the play, which was that, good or bad, the work was a landmark. Even more so, Hernani's characterization of himself added to the interest of the Romantic-minded public:

> *Je suis une force qui va.*
> *Agent aveugle et sourd de mystères funèbres!*
> *Une âme de malheur faite avec des ténèbres!*
> *Où vais-je? je ne sais. Mais je me sens poussé*
> *D'un souffle impétueux, d'un destin insensé.*

Je descends, je descends, et jamais ne m'arrête.
Si parfois, haletant, j'ose tourner la tête,
Une voix me dit: Marche! et l'abîme est profond,
Et de flamme ou de sang je le vois rouge au fond!
Cependant, à l'entour de ma course farouche,
Tout se brise, tout meurt. Malheur à qui me touche!

(I am a driving force, the deaf and blind agent of deadly mysteries, a soul of misfortune made of darkness. Where am I going? I do not know. But I feel myself impelled by a violent gust, by a senseless destiny. I go down, down, and never stop. If sometimes, gasping, I dare turn my head, a voice says, "Go!" and the abyss is deep, and I see it red at the bottom with flame or blood. Meanwhile, around my frightful path, all breaks, dies; let him beware who touches me!)

It is obvious that Hernani is conceived of in a rather different way from Didier. The latter does not think of himself in demonic terms, his temperament is morbid, but not a destructive, driving force. The curious thing about *Hernani*, and the taste it represents, is that all the sinister imagery is centered on the character who is the least sinister of the three major male roles. This kind of displacement provides a tone which immensely pleased audiences, but is somewhat incoherent when we try to analyze it with reference to plot structure. Hernani is a dark force not because of any deeds on his part, but because he was intended to be more interesting that way. Certainly the suicide for *pundonor* at the end of *Hernani* is more a decorative gesture than a cogent denouement. Psychoanalytic criticism, which sometimes gives interesting accounts of peculiar plot structures, can resolve *Hernani* into an Oedipal situation—the King and Don Ruy Gomez being the fathers—but there remains a strong element of improvisation and an attempt at sheer theatrical display to the detriment of overall design.

French critical tradition has it that *Hernani* is totally absurd as motivation and awkward in plot structure, but that the poetry of it somehow transcends all the realities of dramatic construction. For my part, I find that the style of the play is vastly inferior to that of *Cromwell* and *Marion de Lorme*, that the fluency of versification in no way makes up for inappropriate language on the part of the characters, and that the passage quoted above is a good example of the banality of the heightened passages of the play. Hugo wrote *Hernani* in a crisis of needing to reach and please the public, and the language is such as to satisfy spectators not very interested in poetic style and concerned above all with vehemence of feeling. The transformation of Hernani the demon into a grandee and a conspirator in matters of high politics is awkwardly contrived. This brings us to the principal peculiarity of the play in relation to its immediate predecessors. Hugo set it in a time and place of which neither he nor his public had any clear image, of the kind transmitted by literature. Talk of honor makes it "Spanish," of course, a Spain with no particularly characteristic diction, nothing but a show of place names to individualize it for purposes of the play. The manners come from the Gothic novel, not from Hugo's reading of Spanish writers of the sixteenth century. There are, most noticeably, no salient metaphors (a banal use of dark and light is the main trait in figurative language), no bursts of inventiveness in particular tirades. Even Richard B. Grant, who has done a great deal to show how curious mythic patterns recur in Hugo's work, has found little more to observe about *Hernani* than that the tomb scene in Act IV is related to the cave-dungeon theme, the descent to the underworld which often comes forth in Hugo.[1] *Hernani* is unquestionably full of motifs—for example, the horn call of fate by which Don Ruy Gomez summons Hernani to suicide in the last act—that are intimately connected with the processes of Hugo's imagination, but in terms of style and structure it shows the kind of groping which we see in the first decade or so of his career. His second Spanish play, *Ruy Blas*, was to be an especially interesting contrast.

V   Ruy Blas

On grounds of plot it is easy to reduce *Le Roi s'amuse*, *Marie Tudor*, *Lucrèce Borgia*, and *Angelo* to dramas of love and revenge set in the sixteenth century. It has been pointed out that the court jester of *Le Roi s'amuse* resembles Quasimodo, that maternal love in *Lucrèce Borgia* is like paternal love in the preceding play; in short, the prevailing tendency to show that all of Hugo's plays contain variants of the same characters and situations is easily realized in this group of plays, which have received relatively little attention since the 1830's.[2] The fact that they deserve none, by and large, is due, however, more to a stylistic failure than to the result of a repetitious imagination. *Le Roi s'amuse* has a remarkably tight plot compared with *Hernani*, and it is a familiar one in its operatic form, *Rigoletto:* Verdi's librettist stuck very close to the French play, and from the standpoint of cleanness of outline and total thematic coherence the work is outstanding among Hugo's plays.

But again, the play has no distinctive stylistic color: There is historical color of a sort in the use of noble family names, but that does not add up to a historical *feeling* in the text. The prose plays have not even this semblance of stylistic care; their texture bears no relation to that of *Notre-Dame de Paris* or other highly finished examples of Hugo's prose. The unfortunate conclusion is that, probably for the only time in his entire career, Hugo was writing carelessly for gain, without his usual consuming desire to be first and best in some literary genre.

Ruy Blas, on the other hand, was written when the first clamor over Romantic theater was past; it was in a sense gratuitous, Hugo already being an established playwright. It is generally considered his finest play by far from the dramaturgical standpoint: The lucid and precise concatenation of events in the plot is distributed with great skill over five acts and a steady focus is maintained, so that we never have the feeling of bifurcation in the action or irrelevant display in individual scenes. *Ruy Blas* has more in its favor, however, than mere dramatic shape. Its style is that of a much more skillful poet than the Hugo of the earlier plays, its historical color more subtly worked out.

The action of *Ruy Blas* takes place at the end of the seventeenth century in Spain, during the reign of the last, somewhat degenerate Hapsburg king, Charles II, who, in strickly historical terms, left Spain a political shambles, weakened by loss of possessions and a future object of prey for other royal houses. The French court, which ultimately placed its own candidate on the Spanish throne, took considerable interest in the peninsula, and there are French memoirs of Spanish court life of the period, of which Hugo availed himself and which seem to have reinforced his personal memories of the Spanish nobility a century or so later. The theme of the decadence of a society falling apart at the top greatly stimulated Hugo's imagination; the manners of the play, as the historical ambiance used to be called, do not derive from some arbitrary notion of honor, as in *Hernani*, but grow out of the characters being caught in a disintegrating world. No other play of Hugo's has such a rich feeling of time and place, and no other kind of historical coloring seems so suited to his favorite theme of being trapped in a situation and to his favorite device of mask and disguise.

Rather than summarize the action of *Ruy Blas* before discussing it, we shall simultaneously examine plot, character, and style. The opening scene, in an apartment at court, finds Don Salluste packing. "Ruy Blas, close the door and open this window," is the first line, establishing the identity of the latter as a lackey, an object in the hands of Don Salluste. Everyday language used in verse, a favorite idea of Hugo's, is at once flatter and more functional here than in any previous play. The whole denouement is implicit in Ruy Blas's taking orders. Don Salluste then rages at his being dismissed from court for seducing a maid-in-waiting of the Queen's; he addresses his mysterious alter ego Gudiel:

> *Ah! c'est un coup de foudre!... —oui, mon règne est passé,*
> *Gudiel!—renvoyé, disgracié, chassé!—*
> *Ah! tout perdre en un jour!—L'aventure est secrète,*
> *Encor, n'en parle pas.—Oui, pour une amourette,*
> *— Chose, à mon âge, sotte et folle, j'en convien!—*
> *Avec une suivante, une fille de rien!*
> *Séduite, beau malheur! parce que la donzelle*
> *Est à la reine, et vient de Neubourg avec elle,*
> *Que cette créature a pleuré contre moi,*
> *Et traîné son enfant dans les chambres du roi;*
> *Ordre de l'épouser. Je refuse. On m'exile.*
> *On m'exile! Et vingt ans d'un labeur difficile,*
> *Vingt ans d'ambition, de travaux nuit et jour;*
> *Le président haï des alcades de cour,*
> *Dont nul ne prononçait le nom sans épouvante;*
> *Le chef de la maison de Bazan, qui s'en vante;*
> *Mon crédit, mon pouvoir; tout ce que je rêvais*
> *Tout ce que je faisais et tout ce que j'avais,*
> *Charge, emplois, honneurs, tout en un instant s'écroule,*
> *Au milieu des éclats de rire de la foule!*

(Ah! it's a thunderbolt! Yes, my reign has passed, Gudiel!—sent off, disgraced, dismissed! Ah, to lose everything in one day! The adventure is still secret; don't mention it.—Yes, for a little affair—a stupid, foolish thing at my age, I admit—with a maid-in-waiting, a girl of no importance. Seduced, what a tragedy! because the girl is the Queen's, and comes from Neuburg with her, because this creature wept against me, and dragged her child into the royal chambers. An order to marry her; I refuse. I am exiled! And twenty years of hard work, twenty years of ambition, of slaving night and day, the hated president of the court alcades, whose name no one pronounced without terror, the head of the house of Bazan, which was proud of it, my credit, my power, everything I dreamed of, everything I did, and everything I was, position, office, honors, everything falls apart in a second, amidst the crowd's hoots of laughter.)

This opening is very different from that of Hugo's previous plays in two ways. First, it resembles in its direct fullness of detail the beginning of a Neoclassical play. Hugo's dramaturgy is tighter here than it had been before. The kind of uncertain opening situation for which he had earlier been reproached is gone; in its place we have a psychological rather than merely physical *in medias res* situation. Unquestionably the fact that he no longer felt the need to surprise an audience at all costs (as with the hidden staircase at the beginning of *Hernani*) led Hugo to simplify. What is quite startling, however, and not in the least simple by comparison with his earlier work, is the language Don Salluste uses. The use of sentence fragments constitutes a great new liberty with verse style, and the long concluding sentence is constructed in an elliptical fashion: "Twenty years . . . the president . . . everything . . ." Nothing of the sort occurs in earlier plays, where syntax dutifully follows accustomed canons of completeness and clarity. The "broken alexandrine" is no longer merely a matter of enjambment, which Hugo had discussed in the preface to *Cromwell*, but derives from the sentence structure itself. The erratic language of anger had never before found itself so fitting a form in French verse.

The image of an infernal machine and subterranean building or excavation is introduced almost immediately:

> *Oh! mais je vais construire, et sans en avoir l'air,*
> *Une sape profonde, obscure et souterraine . . .*

(I am going to build, without seeming to, a deep, dark, underground mine.)

Endless developments of this imagery are to occur, and unlike its use in previous plays, it does not merely designate a kind of abstract evil destiny, but the very precise machinations of Don Salluste, which end in the sunken chamber of Acts IV and V. *Ruy Blas* is not a play about fate even though the main character will speak of his destiny like Didier or Hernani. Its subject is far more clearly delineated, and its action does not have to be referred to some vague metaphysical entity. Again, by placing the control of the plot squarely in the hands of one character, Don Salluste, Hugo has drawn much closer to the precision of Neoclassical theatrical action, at least in its ideal form.

Don Salluste sets to work immediately at his scheme of revenge, the object of which we gradually understand will be the Queen, who

has banished him. He summons a bizarre figure, his noble cousin
Don César, who lives among the riffraff of Madrid unbeknownst
to the rest of the court, for whom he had merely vanished some years
before. As Don Salluste describes Don César, the rhymes tend to
become witty and unusual:

> *Une marquise*
> *Me disait l'autre jour en sortant de l'église:*
> *—Quel est donc ce brigand qui, là-bas, nez au vent,*
> *Se carre, l'oeil au guet et la hanche en avant,*
> *Plus délabré que Job et plus fier que Bragance,*
> *Drapant sa gueuserie avec son arrogance,*
> *Et qui, froissant du poing sous sa manche en haillons*
> *L'épée à lourd pommeau qui lui bat les talons,*
> *Promène, d'une mine altière et magistrale,*
> *Sa cape en dents de scie et ses bas en spirale?*

(A marquise said to me the other day, as she left church, "Who is that
brigand, who, over there, his nose in the air, struts along, his eye on the
lookout, more squalid than Job and prouder than the house of Braganza,
draping his raggedness in his haughtiness, clutching under his tattered
sleeve the heavy-pommeled sword beating his heels, who displays with an
arrogant, masterful air his unraveling cape and his tumbling stockings?)

Verbal embellishment tends to accompany the appearance of Don
César, who is an entirely new kind of grotesque in Hugo's theater,
a literally daft character who squandered a fortune and maintains
in a life of thievery aristocratic semblances and the cult of honor.
Don César is a comic figure but suggests, like more somber sections
of the play, the background of chaotic decadence of the nobility,
against which the action takes place. Hugo carefully avoids any
direct commentary on Don César as a social symbol; his value as
such is all the more enhanced.

When Don César and Ruy Blas, alone together for a moment,
reveal they are old friends, some further exposition occurs, this time
touching Ruy Blas and his past. He is an orphan nobly educated, or
at least sent to school, through charity, with the privileged. He had
been a wanderer before he became a lackey. It is evident that Hugo
is showing again his desire to make an outsider of his main young
masculine character—his tenor, so to speak. As a kind of picturesque
figure against the background of moldering Spain, Ruy Blas is not
so unrelated to his society as is Didier, or so improbable a *bandito*
as Hernani, whose family quarrels remain as dim as his descent to

highwaymanry. Don César's dropping from his social status, the insistence later on Spain's poverty and disorganization, and the picaresque tradition give some verisimilitude to Ruy Blas's odd position. We may wonder how much the seventeenth-century Spanish *comedia*, with its emphasis on rank and nobility, an emphasis which seems strangely oriented to class conflict for the modern reader, contributed to Hugo's vision of Spanish society in *Ruy Blas*. It is curious that few concrete uses of Spanish literature have been found in Hugo's work—as against endless supposed personal reminiscences of Spain—and it is not out of the question that he rarely mentioned Spanish drama because he found it so congenial and inspiring.

The revelations which Ruy Blas has to make to Don César in the first act are of another order than the purely sociological. In fact, they constitute the meat of the play for psychoanalytic interpretation, and, in this respect, *Ruy Blas* is not only a capital play dramaturgically, but a lucid example of Hugo's imaginings about power, male and female. Ruy Blas tells why he has joined Don Salluste's staff: He is in love with the Queen and his position permits him to see her (Don Salluste overhears this). After much demonic imagery accompanying this revelation (his secret love is poisonous, black, and plunges him into an abyss), there is a transition, written in Hugo's elliptical new style:

> *Je l'attends tous les jours au passage. Je suis*
> *Comme un fou! Oh! sa vie est un tissu d'ennuis,*
> *A cette pauvre femme!—Oui, chaque nuit j'y songe.—*
> *Vivre dans cette cour de haine et de mensonge,*
> *Mariée à ce roi qui passe tout son temps*
> *A chasser! Imbécile!—un sot! vieux à trente ans!*
> *Moins qu'un homme! à régner comme à vivre inhabile.*
> *—Famille qui s'en va.—Le père était débile . . .*

(I wait for her to pass every day. I am like a madman! Oh, her life is a stream of troubles, this poor woman's. Yes, every night I think about it. Living in this court of hate and lying, married to a king who spends all his time hunting. Imbecilic! a fool, old at thirty. Less than a man, incapable of reigning or living. A decaying family. The father was weak . . .)

The melodramatic quality of the lackey's loving a queen can be, of course, translated into male child and mother, and it can be maintained that no other justification exists for the violence of Ruy Blas's exclamation, "I am jealous of the King," since in both the history of royal marriages and the conventions of the play, Carlos is not a threat to a lover. He is even, in the above lines, implied to be impotent. Dismissing of the father in the Freudian Family Romance would seem to be an unconscious motive in a plot structure where king and queen are parents, the lackey a child.[3] As neatly as this kind of analysis fits, however, it is difficult to explain why Hugo, in 1837, should have imagined so Oedipal a plot in comparison with those of his preceding works. And finally, it has been suggested that for an audience in the 1830's there was something genuinely repulsive about lackeys loving queens. Hugo's dramatic effect can be conceived of as coming from the desire to upset accepted social categories as well as from psychoanalytic sources. I leave it to the reader to choose between possible interpretations.

At the end of Act I, which has an elegantly circular structure, Don Salluste gives his final order to Ruy Blas, matching the one in the first line of the play. He orders him, disguised now as a grandee, when the Queen passes, "To charm that woman and be her lover." The second act is an interlude at court: It revolves around the etiquette proper to the Queen of Spain's entourage, and Ruy Blas is guessed to be the Queen's secret admirer. It has always been customary to claim that this or that in Hugo's plays was really unnecessary, as if the machine had superfluous cogs. More so than any other of Hugo's plays, however, *Ruy Blas* is built up so that each act contributes some special element of mood or style. Here it is the fussy court etiquette which sets the tone for the whole act, just as Don Salluste's machinations determine that of the first one. It is important for Hugo to stress the way in which court life is filled with outmoded, obscure usages which make the Queen at once powerful and incapable of doing many simple things. The capricious character of the court is essential to the conception of the great decadence setting in all over Spain, a theme which is finally made explicit at the beginning of Act III, where Ruy Blas addresses the privy council, thanks to his rise at court.

Ruy Blas's apostrophe to the memory of the Emperor Charles V is characteristic of the astringent, violent metaphors he uses in the council scene. They are related in their extravagance to the language used by and about Don César; the comic and the vituperative can be similar. They are of a kind which never previously occur in Hugo's plays and which recall the farfetched, often grotesque conceits of the Baroque period, at the end of which, in Spain, the play takes place. Spain, it must be remembered, saw some of the most extreme examples of Baroque literature, and one wonders to what extent Hugo was aware of the historical appropriateness of this language in a Spanish context:

> *Ton globe, qui brillait dans ta droite profonde,*
> *Soleil éblouissant qui faisait croire au monde*
> *Que le jour désormais se levait à Madrid,*
> *Maintenant, astre mort, dans l'ombre s'amoindrit,*
> *Lune aux trois quarts rongée et qui décroît encore,*
> *Et que d'un autre peuple effacera l'aurore!*
> *Hélas! ton héritage est en proie aux vendeurs.*
> *Tes rayons, ils en font des piastres! Tes splendeurs,*
> *On les souille!—O géant! se peut-il que tu dormes?—*
> *On vend ton sceptre au poids! un tas de nains difformes*
> *Se taillent des pourpoints dans ton manteau de roi;*
> *Et l'aigle impérial, qui, jadis, sous ta loi,*
> *Couvrait le monde entier de tonnerre et de flamme,*
> *Cuit, pauvre oiseau plumé, dans leur marmite infâme!*

(Your orb, which shone in your deep right hand, a dazzling sun which gave the world to believe that henceforth the day rose in Madrid, now, a dead star, shrinks in the shadow, a moon gnawed three quarters away, and still waning, which the dawn of another people will obliterate. Alas, your heritage has fallen to vendors. They make piasters of your beams; they befoul your splendors. O Giant, can you be asleep? Your scepter is being sold by weight; a gang of hideous dwarfs is cutting up your king's mantle into doublets. And the imperial eagle, which, once, under your law, covered the whole world with thunder and fire, is cooking, poor plucked bird, in their vile pot.)

The grotesque occurs here with a new stylistic meaning and force. The images of Spain decaying are placed in a traditionally important location, the beginning of the third act, because the characters are involved very much in a particular moment of history and in a particular society. The monarchy will decay through ill government and the indifference of the noblemen; the characters' lives fall apart because of the false social situations they are in.

The return of Don Salluste, in the later part of Act III, his making Ruy Blas again open and close windows despite his disguise as a grandee, provides the classic reversal of third acts. The fourth, then, merely confuses the situation without advancing the basic donnée: Don Salluste's determination to humiliate the Queen. Don César returns and stumbles about in Don Salluste's "spider web." All this

would be questionable dramaturgy were it not for the special
function of Don César that we have already observed. All the situations in the play are socially out of order, and the reason for this is
the decay of the court, of which Don César is the comic example. His
decline from the nobility, coupled with his legitimate lordly manner,
makes him the perfect character accidentally to upset Don Salluste's
attempt to lure the Queen to his household with a letter inadvertently
written by Ruy Blas. Don César puts on masks more readily than
even Ruy Blas, fully confusing servants and masters alike, as he
temporarily disrupts, with his almost unthinking crazy inventiveness,
the plans of his cousin. For once, the elements of disguise Hugo was
so fond of in his plots has a kind of justification and verisimilitude
in manners.

It Act V is short and follows Neoclassical decorum in many ways.
Don Salluste is killed offstage, after his plot to confront the Queen
with the base birth of her lover has succeeded. Ruy Blas drinks
poison, a noble death and acceptable to stage representation by its
lack of bloodshed. The motivation for the ending is purely psychological and depends on the unsuitability of Ruy Blas's advances to
the Queen, who knows now that he is an adventurer. His choices are
suicide or departure; it matters little except that death represented
the strong basic conformity of Hugo's dramaturgy to handy Neoclassical conventions.

To speak of decorum is again to relate *Ruy Blas* to the traditional
conception of tragedy in France. Conformity is imperfect, of course,
despite the fact that something like the elusive "unity of action,"
to which Hugo professed allegiance in the preface to *Cromwell*,
obtains. Despite also the comic figure of Don César, there is an
amazing unity of tone: The idea of decline is present in all the main
characters: All are caught doing something unbefitting their station,
a station that has been rigidly imposed on them, even though it does
not seem to represent a creative, useful organization of society.
By contrast, Doña Sol in *Hernani* has so vague a noble station that
the impropriety of her conduct hardly distracts the reader. Hugo
spoke in his preface to *Ruy Blas* of *le peuple aspirant aux régions
élevées* as being one interpretation of the play.

It would be wrong, however, to assume from this that the play
embodies a clear social thesis; Hugo intended more to underscore
that there is a natural process of social renewal at work, which is
being thwarted by worn-out social forms. *Ruy Blas* is a political

play in the way Corneille's are: The characters are caught in a large historical scheme. This dimension is lacking in much of Hugo's drama, where an arbitrary sense of honor, a curse, fate, or some convenient and popular device brings the action to its close. Those plays are in a sense reversible in their action: If Didier or Hernani changed his mind about a point of honor in Act V, the whole action would be undone and life would return to normal. *Ruy Blas* could not be turned around in this way. The forces molding its scheme of decorum and the characters' adherence to it have been too well established. It is for this larger kind of coherence, as well as for its remarkable style and tightness of plot, that *Ruy Blas* stands out so in Hugo's dramatic production.

VI   Les Burgraves

Les Burgraves seems in many ways more like an epic fragment or poem given dramatic form, not so much because of its stage-worthiness as because the author simply conceived of it as dialogue. This impression may be unduly influenced by our knowledge that it bored audiences and was a failure. On the other hand, it differs notably from Hugo's previous plays in several primarily theatrical ways. The speeches are often very long; comic characters or interludes are absent; *coups de théâtre* are relatively few in number; the love story which was expected in Romantic drama is subordinate to other interests; and, finally, much of the play is devoted to gradually piecing together the events of the past.

The story is laid in a castle on the Rhine in the thirteenth century, in which four generations of burgraves, or princes, live, each successive generation showing increasing incivility and vicious criminal instincts. We learn from minor characters about the ancient wars of the burgraves led by Job, the oldest living one, against Frederick Barbarossa, the Emperor, as well as how Frederick, raised under the protection of a bastard brother, each ignorant of the other's identity, was almost killed by the latter. There are also predictions about Frederick's return from death and eventual punishment of the bastard. An old hag, Guanhumara, makes a young noble promise, in return for curing his fiancée, to murder a certain unknown Fosco. As a beggar appears asking for shelter, old Job describes himself as the excommunicated outlaw prince of Europe. The beggar reveals himself as Frederick, come back after twenty years of penance for desecrating Charlemagne's tomb, and identifies himself as the younger brother Job had tried to murder. The third and last act takes place in the vault beneath the castle where Job had tried to kill Guanhumara, with whom he was in love, as well as his rival brother. The order to kill Fosco, who is Job, is about to be carried out and is stopped by Frederick, to whom Job has given up his power. The Empire will pass to the would-be young murderer who is in reality Job's son.

The unfolding of the play is probably simpler than a résumé suggests—the reader guesses quickly some of the hidden identities. Thematically what dominates is the image of the two Germanies, that of Job the excommunicated and that of the Emperor, which once existed and which are suddenly brought back to reality by Frederick's appearance. Job says, after submitting to the Emperor:

> —*L'empereur!—Nous étions l'un pour l'autre un fantôme;*
> *Et nous nous regardions d'un oeil presque ébloui*
> *Comme les deux géants d'un monde évanoui!*
> *Nous restons en effet seuls tous deux sur l'abîme;*
> *Nous sommes du passé la double et sombre cime;*
> *Le nouveau siècle a tout submergé; mais ses flots*
> *N'ont point couvert nos fronts, parce qu'ils sont trop hauts!*
> *L'un des deux va tomber. C'est moi. L'ombre me gagne.*
> *O grand événement! chute de ma montagne!*
> *Demain, le Rhin mon père au vieux monde allemand*
> *Contera ce prodige et cet écroulement,*
> *Et comment a fini, rude et fière secousse,*
> *Le grand duel du vieux Job et du vieux Barberousse.*

(The Emperor! We were phantoms for each other, and we looked at each other with dazzled eyes, like the two giants of a vanished world. We remain indeed alone, the two of us, on the edge of the abyss. We are the double and dark peak of the past. The new age has submerged everything, but its waves have not covered our heads because they are too high! One of us will fall; it is I. Shadow overcomes me. O great happening! fall of my mountain! Tomorrow the Rhine, my father, will tell the old German world of this wonder and this collapse and how there ended a proud and violent clash, the great duel of old Job and old Barbarossa.)

The recurrent vertical imagery of giants and castles on mountains is present, but it is coupled with that of submersion and the flow of time which is also characteristic of the play. Hugo is trying to project the mythic idea of a double realm, heaven and hell, which existed in a distant past and now will be reconciled. Cain and Abel are referred to as well as the battle of the Gods and the Titans. The feeling of time is very peculiar in the play: There is an almost mythic past, the time of the great battles, as opposed to a degenerate present, that of the younger burgraves. But this past is like a spell cast over the present, which must be broken so that an era of renewal can take place. The present of the younger burgraves is in a sense less real than the ancient times when Job and Barbarossa fought, before the latter's mysterious disappearance; this is why the characters in the play constantly, obsessively speak of what once happened, as if the Emperor's supposed death had not really resolved the old conflict. This displacement of the feeling of time is perhaps the strangest effect Hugo created in *Les Burgraves*. It is clear that archetypes like the war between the Gods and Titans, the opposing kingdoms of good and evil, were very much in Hugo's mind when he constructed the plot, but the rendering of an atmosphere in which myth is felt as present is something far more complex and original.[4]

The cavern under the castle, where the ancient conflict is resolved and a new age proclaimed, is a prominent example of the archetype of a descent into death and the acquisition of knowledge. The scene is a reenactment of the original source of the conflict, the rivalry over Guanhumara, in that the three characters are present again in the place of the attempted murder, but now, by a reversal, it is the victims who spare Job. The feeling for overt symmetry, for the resolution of opposites through a symbolic act, is characteristic of mythic patterns and helps to make *Les Burgraves* an extremely clear play in its design, despite the impression a résumé may give with its tales of concealed identity. But it is easy to see that this kind of composition, while effective for the reader, would not readily entertain an audience accustomed to more stage "business." With *Les Burgraves* Hugo was already moving toward the kind of narrative found in his later work; he had not yet, save for some juvenilia, attempted any lengthy narrative verse. Casting *Les Burgraves* in the form of a play, and expecting the same audience to enjoy it which had applauded his earlier dramas, came perhaps from the habit of writing verse plays and the fact that he had not yet thought out the possibilities of long narrative poems. In any case, *Les Burgraves* seems a hybrid, owing something to skill at writing for the theater, but already showing the concern for mythic dimensions and design which were to become even more pronounced with the passage of time and which the stage cannot easily accommodate. Some elements in Hugo's private mythology had also begun to appear in his poems of the 1830's, as we shall shortly see.

CHAPTER 4

From Les Feuilles d'automne
to Les Rayons et les Ombres

I *Introduction*

VICTOR Hugo's collections of poems published between 1830 and 1840 usually receive a somewhat biased approach from commentators. The bias lies not necessarily in underestimating their value, though that sometimes happens and is not surprising, given the greater brilliance of his later work. Rather, there is a tendency to see in these volumes some indication of Hugo's attitudes toward politics and society to the exclusion of their more specifically literary qualities. For example, "Fonction du poète" ("The Poet's Function"), a long piece, is often treated as if it represented primarily a new orientation in Hugo's thought, to be found generally in his work of the 1830's, and according to which more personal poetry would be abandoned for verse on public themes. There is a certain truth in this interpretation, but it is only a partial one: The "function of the poet" Hugo is concerned with has literary origins rather than being wholly idiosyncratic. Looking at one stanza, for example, of "Fonction du poète," we can see something beyond a social conception of the poet's role:

> *Si nous n'avions que de tels hommes,*
> *Juste Dieu! comme avec douleur*
> *Le poète au siècle où nous sommes*
> *Irait criant: Malheur! malheur!*
> *On le verrait voiler sa face;*
> *Et, pleurant le jour qui s'efface,*
> *Debout au seuil de sa maison,*
> *Devant la nuit prête à descendre,*
> *Sinistre, jeter de la cendre*
> *Aux quatre points de l'horizon!*

(If we had only such men, just God! with what sorrow the poet in our age would be crying, "Woe, woe!" He would be seen to cover his face, and, lamenting the dying day, standing at the threshold of his house, before already descending night, sinister, cast ashes to the four points of the horizon.)

We recognize in these lamentations and images of mourning an echo of biblical prophecy and a development strikingly in keeping with it. Many poems of this period owe a great deal to Hugo's continued study of the Bible. Furthermore, this use of topics from the prophets constitutes an adumbration of his later work, and that brings us to another problem in his verse of the 1830's. While recognizing the important way in which it prefigures his later manner, we must not treat it solely as a kind of transitional phase, of interest primarily for what it shows us about the ultimate development of Hugo's imagination. I may seem to have done just this, in quoting the above stanza of "Fonction du poète," and it will be necessary to do so in order to form a clear picture of Hugo's poetry as a whole, but at the same time we shall not fail to observe certain qualities of the volumes of the 1830's which are peculiar to them.

To try to summarize the subject matter or individual character of *Les Feuilles d'automne, Les Chants du crépuscule, Les Voix intérieures*, and *Les Rayons et les Ombres* is not an easy matter. Hugo attempted in his prefaces to characterize somewhat each volume—thus *Les Feuilles d'automne* is concerned with personal themes, *Les Chants du crépuscule* with the social upheaval of the new July Monarchy; nature assumes a new importance in *Les Voix intérieures*, and *Les Rayons et les Ombres* is philosophical. But these distinctions blur, and the reader is more aware of the disparateness of each collection than its unity. There is nothing like the thematic organization of *Les Orientales* here, and the reason is doubtless that, Hugo's reputation having been made by the very early 1830's, he felt less need to dazzle the reading public with poetic volumes all of a piece and therefore more unusual. As in the later editions of the *Odes*, the pieces range from the occasional compliment to poems of private, even domestic inspiration, and to ambitious ones addressed to his age and its problems. The liaison he formed with Juliette Drouet in 1833, and which was to last a lifetime, accounts for a fair number of pieces, which are not always the best; the difficulties of her life as an almost sequestered mistress had to be compensated for by generous amounts of verse tribute.

There are certain thematic areas in the four volumes we are considering that can and should be singled out. One is the work of

Bonapartist inspiration, which consists in part of substantial odes. Bonapartism was, for the time being, a lost cause, and it provided Hugo with an almost neutrally patriotic subject matter which was all the dearer to him because it recalled his dead father, to whom he had grown close in the General's later years. The supposedly egalitarian character of Empire society was connected in Hugo's mind with the need for social action in his own time. (The connection between Napoleon and the lower classes can be seen in the curious poem "Regard jeté dans une mansarde" ["Glance into a Garret," *Les Rayons et les Ombres*], in which his memory sustains the humble.) Social action for Hugo at this time meant charity primarily; his desire to improve the lot of the masses was an example of enlightened thought for his day, though the means he conceived for it were characteristically bourgeois and of limited practicality. He felt that faith in God would also succor the poor in adversity. Again in "Regard jeté dans une mansarde" the Empire, oddly identified with a certain religiosity, serves as a counterpoise to the evil temptations of Voltairean irony. Hugo's detestation of Voltaire reached great heights at this period, when, no longer a Catholic, he became more and more concerned in his poetry with the idea of God, whether on occasions of faith or despair. In sum, patriotism, social amelioration, and deity are the three dominants of Hugo's poetry of this period, although religion is of the three the most pervading and the richest in shades of feeling. So succinct a description of his themes tends to make him sound like a worthy Victorian, annoyingly complacent in his convictions. There is an element of this in his work, and it is the reason why many poems are no longer much read. For example, here is a remarkable passage on the poor:

> *Le pauvre alors s'effraye et prie.*
> *L'hiver, hélas, c'est Dieu qui dort.*
> *C'est la faim livide et maigrie*
> *Qui tremble auprès du foyer mort.*
> ("Dieu est toujours là" ["God Is Still There"], *Les Voix intérieures*)

(The pauper then takes fright and prays. Winter, alas, is God sleeping. It is pale and thin hunger trembling beside the dead hearth.)

The images nicely render the feeling of poverty, but almost immediately an angel—charity—appears on the doorstep, and the experience described in the quatrain quoted gives way to an expression of Hugo's convictions about the necessity of good works, and so forth. The difficulty of conveying his fondest beliefs adequately is the besetting problem of much of his verse of the period. We often perceive an alternation within one poem between passages in which the feeling of something is very deftly brought out and others where Hugo is deliberately lofty, looking down from above on his poor people (or children, women, or whatever); the latter verse may be eloquent enough, but we perceive it as rhetorical commentary. (The aforementioned "Regard jeté dans une mansarde" is quite interesting in this respect.) The distinction is not unlike that made in regard to prose fiction between the function of the author as presenter and as judge of his presented world. Ultimately, as we shall see, these disparities in effect are closely connected to problems of poetic diction, which must now be our concern.

II   Classicism and Pastoral

After *Les Orientales* Hugo might have been expected to abandon completely certain formal and stylistic mannerisms of the *Odes*. Such was not at all the case. Hugo had commented unfavorably on the periphrastic Neoclassical style in the preface to *Cromwell*, and in a piece in *Les Contemplations* written in the 1850's he congratulated himself on having liberated poetic vocabulary: "I called the pig by its name"; "The ode, in the embrace of Rabelais, got drunk" ("Réponse à un acte d'accusation" ["Reply to an Accusation"]). While he may have called the pig by its name, the ode, however, or any other lyric form, never, in Hugo's embrace, lost the feeling for the levels of style. (Even in his dramas, as we have seen and as he indirectly admits in the preface to *Cromwell*, the language is never "lower" than Molière's broadest diction.) Least of all was a Rabelaisian inventiveness of peculiar words Hugo's forte, either in poems or plays. On the contrary, Hugo kept so strong a feeling for the traditional canons of poetic language that many poems of the 1830's seem to represent a regression in stylistic freedom from *Les Orientales*. The Bonapartist odes, in particular, are surprisingly full of periphrases, "veils" (an all-purpose Neoclassical term), "steeds," "domes" (that is, sky), "lyres," and "chariots." To be sure, the language is not as contorted as the examples we have seen from the *Odes*, but neither is it as precise, as free of conventional metonymies, as that of *Les Orientales*. Hugo was still deeply influenced by the poetic bric-a-brac of tradition, and, significantly, none of the poems in Neoclassical diction and form (successions of complicated stanzas, often changing in the course of many subdivisions) survive as anything more than curious examples of Hugo's political beliefs of the period. On the other hand, a new influence, genuinely Classical rather than Neoclassical, that of Virgil, makes itself felt in a certain number of poems.[1]

Hugo seems to have more deeply absorbed at least some areas of Latin poetry than any of the other French Romantics, and in the 1830's the presence of Virgil is especially noticeable in his work. Mythology returns, despite his early condemnation of it under the influence of Chateaubriand, and the slighting references to it in the preface to *Cromwell*. In "A. M. Louis B." (*Les Feuilles d'automne*) two great lines from the *Aeneid* serve as a point of departure for a meditation on the death of Hugo's father:

> *Hic tibi mortis erant metae, domus alta sub Ida*
> *Lyrnesi domus alta, solo Laurente sepulchrum.* (XII, 546–47)

(This was the end set for your death. You had a high dwelling at the foot of Mount Ida, a high dwelling at Lyrnesus, but your tomb lies in Laurentian soil.)

Hugo's father's house in Blois and his grave in Paris become the corresponding places in his poem:

> *Ainsi du vétéran par la guerre épargné,*
> *Rien ne reste à son fils, muet et résigné,*
> *Qu'un tombeau vide, et toi, la maison orpheline*
> *Qu'on voit blanche et carrée au bas de la colline,*
> *Gardant, comme un parfum dans le vase resté,*
> *Un air de bienvenue et d'hospitalité!*

(Thus nothing remains of the veteran, spared by war, for his son, silent and resigned, but an empty tomb, and you, the orphan house that we see white and square at the bottom of the hill, keeping, like scent remaining in a vase, a look of welcome and hospitality.)

A vision of the Acheron and the Elysian fields concludes the poem which had started merely as a description of the house in the Loire valley. Hugo has very gradually introduced the Virgilian correspondences suggested by the epigraph:

> *Ses fils ont déposé sa cendre auprès des leurs,*
> *Afin qu'en l'autre monde, heureux pour les meilleurs,*

Il puisse converser avec ses frères d'armes.
Car sans doute ces chefs, pleurés de tant de larmes,
Ont là-bas une tente. Ils y viennent le soir
Parler de guerre; au loin dans l'ombre, ils peuvent voir
Flotter de l'ennemi les enseignes rivales;
Et l'empereur au fond passe par intervalles.

(His sons have placed his ashes beside theirs, so that in the other world, a happy one for the best, he can converse with his brothers in arms. For doubtless these chiefs, lamented with so many tears, have there a tent. They come there in the evening to speak of war; in the distance, in the shadow, they can see the rival insignia of the enemy and the emperor pass occasionally in the background.)

The mythological material has grown out of the reference to General Hugo's career under the Empire and is not at all the kind of periphrastic, ornamental use of myth customary in Neoclassical poetry. The Virgilian allusions have a complex appropriateness: First, the deserted house and empty tomb serve as a superficial transformation of the dwelling in Lyrnesus and the Laurentian—Italian—grave, but more subtly the theme of death in exile, which is what Virgil's lines are actually about, represents the sad conclusion to the General's career, his separation from army, honors, and Empire in the figurative exile of the Restoration. This side of Hugo's father's life is never explicitly stated in the poem, although we know from other pieces (see the end of "A l'Arc de triomphe" ["To the Arch of Triumph"]) that Hugo was extremely conscious of it and pained by it; the Latin epigraph with its implications colors the meaning of Hugo's lines.

Elsewhere, as in "A Virgile" (*Les Voix intérieures*), the Latin influence can be strongly felt in passages on nature. Hugo's experience of nature often shows the mediation of the *Bucolics* and *Georgics* in choice of detail and vocabulary:

Le vers qu'à moitié fait j'emporte en mon esprit
Pour l'achever aux champs avec l'odeur des plaines
Et l'ombre du nuage et le bruit des fontaines.
("Sagesse" ["Wisdom"], *Les Rayons et les Ombres*)

(The line which, half written, I carry off in my mind to finish in the fields with the odor of the plains and the shadow of the cloud and the sound of springs.)

The recurrent use of general terms, vales, grottoes, shaded woods, and especially the classical sounding *fontaines,* suggests a mind for whom the literary tradition of pastoral, with its moral connotations of uncorruptedness, has a greater hold than the actual detail of real country life or landscapes. Hugo's fields and groves certainly have none of the intricate detail of much English nature poetry. When we find striking images of nature in Hugo, ones which seem quite divorced from pastoral, they tend to be of light and the sky:

> *L'Océan par moments abaissait sa voix haute,*
> *Et moi je croyais voir, vers le couchant en feu,*
> *Sur sa crinière d'or passer la main de Dieu.*

("Ce qu'on entend sur la montagne" ["What You Hear on a Mountain"], *Les Feuilles d'automne*)

(The ocean at moments lowered its loud voice, and I thought I saw, toward the fiery west, the hand of God pass over its golden mane.)

Hugo's biographers have seldom been able to trace any precise relation between his many vacations in the country and the images of his nature poetry. Indeed, it is established that one of the more vivid nature pieces of *Les Feuilles d'automne,* "Dicté en présence du glacier du Rhône" ("Dictated Before the Rhone Glacier"), concerns a landscape Hugo had never seen. Hugo's imagination seems to have functioned with very little of the kind of stimulus of a particular moment and experience of nature we find in the English Romantic poets, and, as we look further into the development of new strains of diction in his poetry of the 1830's, we shall see how remote their tendencies are from the rural.

III   *Figurative Language and Stylistic Coherence*

In "Sagesse," from which we have quoted lines in Hugo's Virgilian manner, there occurs a passage which contrasts sharply with it in style. God is being addressed:

> *Livre et prêtre sont morts. Et la foi maintenant,*
> *Cette braise allumée à ton foyer tonnant,*
> *Qui, marquant pour ton Christ ceux qu'il préfère aux autres,*
> *Jadis purifiait la lèvre des apôtres,*
> *N'est qu'un charbon éteint dont les petits enfants*
> *Souillent ton mur avec des rires triomphants!*

(Book and priest are dead. And now faith, that ember lit in your thundering hearth, which, designating for your Christ those he preferred to others, once purified the lips of the apostles, is now only a dead piece of coal with which little children dirty your wall in triumphant laughter.)

This complicated metaphor, in which a figurative ember turns into a real lump of coal with which children scribble on church walls, demonstrates Hugo's increasing tendency not only to use elaborate tropes, but also the commonplace and trivial in conjunction with the grandiose. Hugo's imagery has become intermittently less "poetic" than in *Les Orientales*, and his indifference to mingling tones is more pronounced. We often notice this in the more urban poems, for, like Sainte-Beuve and before Baudelaire, Hugo began to evoke more and more frequently the atmosphere of the city. Sometimes the diction drops to the conversational, as in "Rêverie d'un passant à propos d'un roi" ("Reverie of a Passerby in Regard to a King," *Les Feuilles d'automne*), where an intentionally flat, casual opening introduces the picture of carriages passing into the courtyard of the Louvre and a gaping crowd; an old woman exclaiming, *Un roi, sous l'empereur, j'en ai tant vu, des rois* (the syntax is most colloquial) leads to a meditation, gradually heightened, on the sea of time and kings:

Le sol toujours s'en va, le flot toujours s'élève.
Malheur à qui le soir s'attarde sur la grève,
Et ne demande pas au pêcheur qui s'enfuit
D'ou vient qu'à l'horizon on entend ce grand bruit!
Rois, hâtez-vous! rentrez dans le siècle où nous sommes,
Quittez l'ancien rivage!—A cette mer des hommes
Faites place, ou voyez si vous voulez périr
Sur le siècle passé que son flot doit couvrir!

Ainsi ce qu'en passant avait dit cette femme
Remuait mes pensers dans le fond de mon âme,
Quand un soldat soudain, du poste détaché,
Me cria:—Compagnon, le soleil est couché.

(The ground steadily vanishes, the waves constantly rise. Woe to him who in the evening remains on the strand, and does not ask the fleeing fisherman why, on the horizon, that great roar is heard. Kings, hurry, come into our age, leave the old shore! Make place for this sea of men, or see if you wish to perish on the past age that its wave will cover. Thus, what the woman said in passing was stirring up my thoughts in the depths of my soul, when a soldier, suddenly, standing off from the sentry box, shouted to me, "You there, the sun has set.")

There is a nice contrast between the swelling tone of the passage on the sea (a metaphor which had been casually introduced early in the poem) and the guard's plain warning that the gates are to be closed. Again, the movement from figurative to concrete is present, as the approach of night over the ocean becomes the real sundown in Paris, with its implications of the end of a royal house. Here Hugo has managed with great success the drop in tone and the juxtaposition of the rhetorical and colloquial.

As Hugo's language grew richer in verbal resources, the problem of blending together various kinds of style into a coherent whole became a crucial one in his poetry. We have seen two utterly different kinds of writing in our quotations from "Sagesse." Admittedly it is a long poem, but some question remains of total effect, and Hugo was not always successful in preventing local effect from overwhelming the feeling of a stylistically organized whole. The new virtues of his poetry of the 1830's—notably striking, elegantly developed metaphors—sometimes militate against the feeling of unity of conception. Now and then an image seems more clever than appropriate, such as this line concluding the somewhat insipid description of a forbiddingly beautiful woman: *Car le baril de poudre a peur de l'étincelle* ("A Ol.," *Les Voix intérieures*). The conceit does not suit the vaporous preceding passage. Other examples of disparity can be found in much better lines in much better poems, but their common denominator is the impression that Hugo has yielded too quickly to a new poetic idea, so that an abstract style may brusquely be juxtaposed with a highly descriptive passage, a plain one with intricate imagery. The readers of the 1830's who disliked Hugo's poetry found it neologistic (by which they meant new figurative uses of words as well as new words), and it was compared with decadent Silver Age Latin verse for the gaudiness of its effects. Today we no longer feel the "neologistic" character of Hugo's diction, but it is possible still to discern the sometimes extreme variations in style which seemed the mark of decadence. Passing without transition from one tone to another was, of course, to be much exploited by poets later in the nineteenth century, and occasionally it occurs impressively in Hugo,

such as at the end of "Rêverie d'un passant . . . ," but more often
in his work of the 1830's it seems haphazard when it occurs.

The fact that Hugo's style was evolving in several ways simultaneously, his development of a pastoral Virgilian style, colloquial
diction, highly wrought metaphor, and bluntly commonplace
urban images, to mention only tendencies we have seen so far,
does not perhaps in itself account entirely for the growing problem
of evenness of texture in his work; there is an element of formal
organization which probably also contributed to shifts of manner
within individual poems. Before the 1830's the use of the alexandrine couplet in works of some lyric pretensions was rather
circumscribed both in French poetry of the late Neoclassical phase
and in Hugo's work in particular. Stanzas were generally felt to be
appropriate to loftiness of inspiration. The habit of writing alexandrine couplets for the stage may have contributed to the increasing
importance of the form in Hugo's work after 1830; in any case, a
large proportion of the volumes under consideration consists of
poems in couplets arranged in verse paragraphs. The freedom of
verse paragraphs as opposed to stanzas was an invitation to build
up pieces of somewhat looser apparent structure than was customary
in stanzas. As a result, very new effects in juxtaposition of subject
matter or development of subject became possible for Hugo, who
excelled over all his contemporaries in constructing such poems.
The meditative poem with subtle shifts benefited especially from
the arrangement in verse paragraphs. Transitions could be omitted,
continuity merely implied, and concluding sections added which
would serve primarily to set a cadential mood rather than reach an
ending in any logical sequence. The following lines exemplify this
new function of the verse paragraph:

> Amas sombre et mouvant de méditations!
> Problèmes périlleux! obscures questions
> Qui font que, par moments s'arrêtant immobile,
> Le poète pensif erre encor dans la ville
> A l'heure où sur ses pas on ne rencontre plus
> Que le passant tardif aux yeux irrésolus
> Et la ronde de nuit, comme un rêve apparue,
> Qui va tâtant dans l'ombre à tous les coins de rue!

("Il n'avait pas vingt ans . . ."["He Was Not Yet Twenty"], *Les Chants du
crépuscule*)

(Dark and moving mass of meditations! Perilous problems! Obscure
questions which cause the poet, at times stopping motionless, still to wander

pensively in the city, at the hour when on his way he encounters no one
except the tardy passerby with uncertain eyes, and the nightwatch, appearing
like a dream, groping in the shadows at every corner.)
The meditation preceding these lines has to do with chaotic changes
in society. The image of darkness is, of course, fitting for a poem of
questioning and doubt, but its principal purpose is to provide a
quiet resting point. It is obvious, however, that this method of
constructing poems in discrete sections lends itself to piecing
together stylistically disparate passages, and we often find that
discontinuity in diction occurs precisely in those poems which are
made of verse paragraphs separated at times by asterisks or similar
strong indications of a break. The example we have already used
to illustrate both Virgilian style and metaphoric brilliance,
"Sagesse," is put together in just this fashion.
   We have suggested the probable role of the alexandrine couplet
in verse paragraphs in the stylistic peculiarities of Hugo's poetic
texture, but it would not do to imply that assembling poems of
pieces of various inspiration is the only or ultimately the most
important source of the shifts in diction. Hugo's increasing discovery
of the possibilities of metaphor—and, to a lesser extent, simile—are
surely the deeper cause for them. Hugo stands out among all his
contemporaries of the 1830's for his command of figurative language,
something which they did not fail to comment on. However, the
placing of imagistic high points in his poems often leaves something
to be desired: Remarkable effects can be followed by language which
represents an unfunctional and disappointing drop:

> *Ces temps sont passés.—A cette heure,*
> *Heureux pour quiconque m'effleure,*
> *Je suis triste au dedans de moi.*
> *J'ai sous mon toit un mauvais hôte;*
> *Je suis la tour splendide et haute*
> *Qui contient le sombre beffroi.*
> . . . .
> *L'espoir mène à des portes closes.*
> *Cette terre est pleine de choses*
> *Dont nous ne voyons qu'un côté.*
> ("A Mademoiselle J.," *Les Chants du crépuscule*)

(Those times have passed. Now, happy seeming to anyone who brushes
by me, I am sad inside. I have an evil guest under my roof; I am the splendid

high tower containing the dark belfrey . . . . Hope leads to closed doors.
This earth is full of things of which we see only one side.)

The inventiveness of the language dwindles off gradually after the
unusual image of the tower. All in all, the passage is far more elegant
in its figures of speech than what we find generally in Lamartine,
Sainte-Beuve, Vigny, or Gautier, but the talent for local effect is
misspent or unevenly spent; the sustaining power is lacking.

IV   Prosody and Grammar

At this point it is necessary to discuss in some detail the other
way in which Hugo surpassed his contemporaries and set new
standards for French poetry: versification and poetic syntax. This
will entail some rather technical considerations, but they are
necessary to understanding the peculiar role Hugo played in the
changing character of French poetry in the nineteenth century.

It is relatively easy to write alexandrines which consist of one
sentence or couplets which contain a sentence. The ear readily
tests such constructions; no subtlety of rhythmic sense is involved.
More sophisticated versification comes with the building up of
long sentences over several couplets. High Neoclassical style, such
as we find it in Racine or Corneille, accomplishes this by multipli-
cation of subordinate clauses. However, the rather spare use of
modifying elements—adjectival or adverbial—in the sentence gives
relatively little flexibility in making lines in fairly normal word
order, with the result that inversion of prepositional phrases
(*De ses obscurs complots/C'est donc la triste fin*) becomes one of its
characteristics. A reaction against overfrequent inversion occurs
in the Romantic poets; Hugo singled out this device for ridicule
in the preface to *Cromwell*. Enjambment can lessen the need for it,
although Hugo never abandoned the really expressive use of inversion. It would be wrong, however, if we assumed that by avoiding
the artifice of inversion whenever it seemed idle, Hugo meant poetic
syntax to follow the order of prose. A quite new approach to sentence
patterns in verse arose in the nineteenth century, and Hugo was the
first great exploiter of it. We have seen in examples from *Ruy Blas*
how Hugo broke up normal syntactic patterns into fragments when
necessary to render some of the flavor of spoken language. That is
not, however, the main tendency of his poetic language; rather,
Hugo preferred in his lyric work a new kind of highly developed

syntax which bears little relation to that of Neoclassical practice.
The concluding section of "Que la musique date du seizième siècle"
("That Music Dates from the Sixteenth Century," *Les Rayons et
les Ombres*), a piece devoted to Palestrina and his contribution to
polyphony, will serve as a particularly apt passage for the analysis
of Hugo's syntactic imagination (to say nothing of the remarkable
metaphor involved):

> *Heureux ceux qui vivaient dans ce siècle sublime*
> *Où, du génie humain dorant encor la cime,*
> *Le vieux soleil gothique à l'horizon mourait!*
> *Où déjà, dans la nuit emportant son secret,*
> *La cathédrale morte en un sol infidèle*
> *Ne faisait plus jaillir d'églises autour d'elle!*
> *Ere immense obstruée encore à tous degrés,*
> *Ainsi qu'une Babel aux abords encombrés,*
> *De donjons, de beffrois, de flèches élancées,*
> *D'édifices construits pour toutes les pensées;*
> *De génie et de pierre énorme entassement;*
> *Vaste amas d'où le jour s'en allait lentement!*
> *Siècle mystérieux où la science sombre*
> *De l'antique Dédale agonisait dans l'ombre*
> *Tandis qu'à l'autre bout de l'horizon confus,*
> *Entre Tasse et Luther, ces deux chênes touffus,*
> *Sereine, et blanchissant de sa lumière pure*
> *Ton dôme merveilleux, ô sainte architecture,*
> *Dans ce ciel, qu'Albert Dure admirait à l'écart,*
> *La musique montait, cette lune de l'art!*

(Happy they who lived in that sublime age when, still gilding the heights
of human genius, the old Gothic sun was dying on the horizon; when,
already bearing away its secret into the night, the cathedral, dead in faithless
soil, no longer made churches burst forth around it! An immense era, still
obstructed at all levels, like a Tower of Babel with clutter about it, by turrets,
belfries, slim spires, edifices built for all thoughts—an enormous heap of genius and stone. Great mass from which the sun slowly withdrew! Mysterious
age, when the somber science of ancient Daedalus lay dying in the shadow,
while, at the other end of the murky horizon, between Tasso and Luther,
those thick-leafed oaks, serene and making glow with its pure light your
enchanted dome, O holy architecture, in that sky which Albrecht Dürer
secretly wondered at, there arose music, the moon of art!)

The whole development hangs on the elliptical, if traditional,
formula of the first line: "Happy they who . . . " (The Latinate

character of the expression is not without significance, as we shall see.) At first the *où* clauses develop the thought in the syntactic manner of Neoclassical rhetoric, except that the present participles—far denser than relative clauses—are more characteristic of the new kind of epithetical style. Shortly, however, with "ère immense," there begins a series of appositions, some of which, like "vaste amas ... ," are not absolutely clear in their precise grammatical reference, or else might be taken simply as exclamations. The *tandis que* clause is a clever hinge phrase, typical of nineteenth-century descriptive writing, which permits the imagery to reach its full development without any prosaic break in sentence structure, such as "but" or "however" would have introduced. With the image of the oaks we encounter a very pure form of the apposition as metaphor, as opposed to the apposition as explanation; this kind of apposition is a most characteristic device of Hugo's, especially since it can be placed very freely in the word order and need not necessarily follow its reference as here. A striking displacement of word order occurs in the next line with "sereine," which is separated in almost Latinate fashion from "musique," which it modifies. Furthermore, the position of "sereine" at the beginning of a line illustrates a very typical device in Hugo; the first syllables of the alexandrine are treated with the emphasis they might have in a more inflected language where total freedom of word order allows the key term place of precedence. Adjectives, present participles, and appositions can all be considered kinds of epithets, to use a more rhetorical than grammatical term, and Hugo's verse is infinitely richer than that of his contemporaries in the variety and placement of these epithets. The degree to which Latin influenced him in his devising of new kinds of word order cannot be assessed with absolute certainty. Suffice it to say, however, that the extent to which Hugo imitated or quoted Latin poetry throughout his life suggests a knowledge of it which, if not that of a professional classicist, was deep and thorough within its limits.

The abundant use of appositions and epithets suggests the ever increasingly nominal character of Hugo's style, which corresponds to the general tendency of nineteenth-century French poetry. But the fondness for adjectival constructions did not lead in other poets to the same kind of handling of the apposition as metaphor which we see in the last line of our quotation. The syntactical condensation which this permits—there are no "like's" or "as's" needed, nor "of" constructions, such as *la lune de la musique*—leads toward a new density of image. Condensation of figurative language with an attendant emphasis on noun syntax marks most of the great stylistic innovators after Hugo among the nineteenth-century poets. His example, more than any other, proved seminal for poets who in tone and theme do not resemble him, but who were able, on the technical level of poetic syntax, to profit by his example. Rimbaud and Mallarmé, to name only two remarkable examples, developed, each in his own way, the appositional metaphor.

V   *Visionary Poems*

In the conclusion to "Que la musique . . ." we found, in addition to elegance of syntactic elaboration, an analogy which runs completely contrary to the usual clichés about the "dark" ages and the dawn of the Renaissance. The other passages we have quoted so far tend to make striking use of contrasts of dark and light, often subtle or unexpected. This kind of metaphor points toward the most characteristic imagery of Hugo's later work. Much the same may be said for the comparison of Tasso and Luther to oak trees with heavy foliage. These oaks are not unlike the forest in "A Albert Dürer" (*Les Voix intérieures*), "horrible," "monstrous," "visionary." The Virgilian pastoral we have seen is counterbalanced in Hugo's work by a convulsive, nightmarish, often crepuscular landscape: *Une forêt pour toi* [Dürer] *c'est un monde hideux*. Dürer's name occurs almost as frequently as Virgil's in Hugo's poems of the 1830's,[2] and the vision Hugo derived from his work, like the Virgilian one, represents his tendency to see nature in a form mediated by art rather than in the fashion of an English nature poet. The Dürer landscape is further associated with Piranesi's fantastic architectural drawings and the recurrent theme of Babel, a monstrous citadel. Hugo saw in many ways much more with the inner eye, and the strange, fascinating drawings—many of them bordering on the surrealistic—which he began to make in the late 1830's demonstrate his peculiar gift of turning what he saw into some private vision quite remote from the object itself. The kind of panic vision of strange edifices and monstrously distorted features of landscape which was later to occupy his mind was beginning to emerge. Gothic architecture already played a definitely sinister-fantastic role in *Notre-Dame de Paris*, as it does in the lines we have quoted from "Que la musique . . ." The *effrayantes Babels que rêvait Piranèse* are already present in "La Pente de la rêverie" ("The Incline of Reverie," *Les Feuilles d'automne*): This is a strange poem, much admired in recent decades, in which, looking out the window, the poet sees a deep, whirling, spiral-shaped vision, a phantasmagoria with, at its nether end, eternity.

"Puits de l'Inde . . ." ("India's Wells," *Les Rayons et les Ombres*), a description evidently from engravings of the Hindu underground temples, is an even better-developed example of the new visionary mode:

> *Puits de l'Inde! tombeaux! monuments constellés!*
> *Vous dont l'intérieur n'offre aux regards troublés*
> *Qu'un amas tournoyant de marches et de rampes,*
> *Froids cachots, corridors où rayonnent des lampes,*
> *Poutres où l'araignée a tendu ses longs fils,*
> *Blocs ébauchant partout de sinistres profils,*
> *Toits de granit, troués comme une frêle toile,*
> *Par où l'oeil voit briller quelque profonde étoile,*
> *Et des chaos de murs, de chambres, de paliers,*
> *Où s'écroule au hasard un groupe d'escaliers!*

(Wells of India! tombs! star-studded monuments! You whose inside shows the worried glance only a whirling heap of steps and ramps, cold dungeons, corridors where lamps shine, beams where the spider has stretched its long threads, blocks everywhere suggesting sinister profiles, granite roofs pierced like a filmy cloth, through which the eye sees some deep star shine, and chaos of walls, rooms, landings, where haphazardly a group of stairflights crumbles!)

Many key words are here: those pertaining to staircases, prison, spider webs, walls, and interstices through which light can be glimpsed. These are symbols of fate, as Hugo makes explicit at the end of the piece. I confess to finding the visionary poems of the 1830's more interesting as examples of constants of Hugo's imagination than as works of art in themselves. Their symbolism is already present in germ in *Notre-Dame de Paris*, their diction somewhat dry compared with the metaphoric elegance we have seen elsewhere. Hugo's fascination with labyrinthine architectural motifs can be precious to the psychoanalytically oriented critic who finds in them sinister symbols of the female. These poems also demonstrate a continuity in Hugo's imagination which those who first wrote on him did not always see. At the same time, since our concern is with Hugo's work as finished examples of poetry, there is no reason to give undue emphasis to them, since they lack the brilliance and color of the later visions in the same vein. To suggest equitably what we should read in Hugo's poetry from *Les Feuilles d'automne* to *Les Rayons et les Ombres,* it will not do to propose only those poems like "A Albert Dürer" or "La Pente de la rêverie," which seem to prefigure Hugo's later style. On the other hand, there is no point in pretending that the Napoleonic odes—or the other political ones—have any particular aesthetic interest merely because they document Hugo's shifting political allegiances. Much is to be found in the poems of the 1830's which is worthy of note in its own right. "Regard jeté dans une mansarde," which we have alluded to, is a good case—eloquent, graceful in shifts of style, and built up of skillfully arranged sections—of Hugo's most finished manner. The same poem, however, concludes with a section addressed by the poet "to himself," which gives the measure of the strength and weaknesses of these poems. We feel a distance between the voice of the poet and his subject, a disparity in language between swelling rhetoric and neat precision. A certain blending and continuity between object and commentary is lacking, and we feel Hugo's absence of control in transitions, his readiness to yield to magniloquence even when the occasion is inappropriate. Hugo's later poetry will tend to correct this imbalance; his sense of stylistic whole will be greater.

CHAPTER 5

Invective, Prophecy, and Vision

I *Exile and* Châtiments

H UGO published no volumes of poetry between *Les Rayons et les Ombres* (1840) and *Châtiments* (1853). He did, of course, write *Les Burgraves* during this period, as well as *Le Rhin* (1842; expanded, 1844), which suggests the sources of that play. *Le Rhin* is considered by a number of critics to be one of Hugo's most appealing works; it is indeed a quite interesting account of the poet's travels in the Rhineland with its medieval cities and impressive feudal ruins. I do not think, however, that the Rhineland experience added anything to the basic données of Hugo's imagination. The story of the Mäuserturm, or Rat Tower, has been adduced as a significant intensification of the nexus of themes of physical mutilation and sinister architecture, but Quasimodo and Notre Dame already exemplified them quite adequately. The trips to Germany seem more a confirmation and an enrichment of the imagery already present in Hugo's work.

After the vacations in Germany came an attempt to rediscover Spain—surely the sign of one whose inspiration has flagged and is searching again for its sources. But this trip ended sadly, and the account of it was not published in Hugo's lifetime. The mournful event was the accidental death by drowning, during his absence, of Hugo's eldest child, Léopoldine, and, while Hugo's reaction to it at the time did not immediately have any greater effect on his poetry than the composition of a few elegiac pieces, its ultimate consequences seem to have been considerable, as we shall see.

In the later 1840's, as a Peer of France and then as an elected member of the assembly formed to found the Second Republic, Hugo had a genuine political career, which can be variously assessed, but which gave him the occasion for public pronouncements which he had doubtless always desired. His political situation during the Republic is a complicated matter: He had been a partisan of the July Monarchy but welcomed the arrival of Louis Napoleon on the political scene. The latter, however, came to be a target of

84

Hugo's vituperations as the Government began to support the papacy's temporal pretensions. Hugo even founded a newspaper, *L'Evénement,* to express his views. But the papal claims were surely not the real issue, and it would be difficult to explain Hugo's attitudes in terms of purely ideological convictions. Once again, psychoanalytic criticism is valuable in the attempt to account for Hugo's reckless vilification of Louis Napoleon—the future Emperor Napoleon III. An elimination, a destruction of a false father figure—Louis Napoleon masquerading as a true Bonaparte—seems to have been at work here. In any case, Hugo rather more than less provoked his exile at the time of the coup d'état of December 2, 1851—the anniversary of the great Napoleon's victory at Austerlitz—and he left France for an incomparably greater destiny than the rather shallow, mundane one which had been his lot and choice during the 1840's.

Hugo's first reaction to exile was to write polemics against Louis Napoleon, *Histoire d'un crime,* which could not be published until the fall of the Empire, and *Napoléon le petit,* which appeared in Brussels in 1852. His return to verse the same year took at first the form of a projected volume, *Les Contemplations,* which would be divided into "pure" poetry, "Autrefois" ("Bygone Days"), and satire, "Aujourd'hui" ("Today"). Of course the invectives of "Aujourd'hui" shortly became the volume of *Châtiments,* and the twofold division of *Les Contemplations* was to mean something quite different when that collection finally came out four years later. This question of planning and arranging his verse is of great importance, however. It recurred frequently in the 1850's, as long pieces or groups of poems were shifted from one plan to another. This means, of course, that there are often close links between works which were published separately and that we must not neglect the unity of inspiration they share.

Châtiments is probably less read than the other collections Hugo published at the height of his powers in the 1850's. The idea of some six thousand lines devoted to castigating the Second Empire tends to put the reader off, and there is no doubt that the attention flags in the course of some of the longer pieces. Nonetheless, *Châtiments* has a number of merits, not the least of which is a consistency of style within each poem, which distinguishes Hugo's later work from that of the 1830's. Furthermore, the volume is something more complex than sustained invective or satire in the traditional sense.

Juvenal is often mentioned in *Châtiments*:

> *Toi qu'aimait Juvénal, gonflé de lave ardente,*
> *Toi dont la clarté luit dans l'oeil fixe de Dante,*
> *Muse Indignation! viens, dressons maintenant,*
> *Dressons sur cet empire heureux et rayonnant,*
> *Et sur cette victoire au tonnerre échappée,*
> *Assez de piloris pour faire une épopée!*

(You whom Juvenal, filled with burning lava, loved, you whose light shines in Dante's staring eye, Muse of Indignation! come, let us erect, over this happy, beaming empire and this victory saved from thunderous wrath, enough pillories to make an epic!)

This passage, the invocation at the end of the first poem, "Nox," is interesting in a number of respects. Dante and Juvenal were abiding inspirations for Hugo, but whereas his conception of Dante was one-sided, his understanding of Juvenal was profound, and he ranked the Roman poet very high on his list of great geniuses. Juvenalian satire can be considered as the model for many poems in *Châtiments:* They move from figure to figure, insulting, mocking, and raging. As in the traditional satire of the Roman type, the scene is crowded with characters, the poem often static in that the satire does not foresee any change in the ugly world it flagellates. The interest of this kind of poetry depends, of course, on its power to transcend the object of its indignation—which the reader may have few feelings about, as is the case of Second Empire politicians—by means of verbal art. In other words, satire cannot work in the way it ostensibly does, for then its interest would be local and transitory. Richness of verbal texture allows satire to convey its mood long after its object has vanished. Many pieces in *Châtiments* remain entertaining even when the reader, who must have fairly full notes in order to follow them in the proper historical context, cannot immediately identify the butt of satire:

> *Ce Zoïle cagot naquit d'une Javotte.*
> *Le diable,—ce jour-là Dieu permit qu'il créât,—*
> *D'un peu de Ravaillac et d'un peu de Nonotte*
> *Composa ce gredin béat.* ("Un Autre" ["Another"])

(This sanctimonious Zoilus was born from a Javotte. The devil—God allowed him to do the creating that day—out of a bit of Ravaillac and a bit of Nonotte, fashioned this smug scoundrel.)

Zoilus was a critic of great ferocity; Javotte designates a peasant girl; Ravaillac murdered Henry IV, and Nonotte was Voltaire's adversary. However, the unexpected rhymes and ludicrous-sounding names are sufficient means of establishing the invective tone without the details always being clear. The range of Hugo's diction is expanded also by abundant historical references, especially to the Roman Empire. Circus images are perhaps the most frequent way Hugo describes the *Empire à grand spectacle* set up by Louis Napoleon, but there are also interesting ones of great violence and gore to complement the purely comic effects:

> *La nature ne put me calmer. L'air, la plaine,*
> *Les fleurs, tout m'irritait; je frémissais devant*
> *Ce monde où je sentais ce scélérat vivant.*
> *Sans pouvoir m'apaiser je fis plus d'une lieue.*
> *Le soir triste monta sous la coupole bleue;*
> *Linceul frissonnant, l'ombre autour de moi s'accrut;*
> *Tout à coup la nuit vint, et la lune apparut*
> *Sanglante, et dans les cieux, de deuil enveloppée,*
> *Je regardai rouler cette tête coupée.* (VII, 5)

(Nature could not calm me. The air, the plain, flowers, everything irritated me. I was trembling in the face of this world where I felt that scoundrel to be alive. Without being able to calm down I walked more than a league; sad night rose up under the blue dome; like a quivering shroud the shadows thickened around me. Suddenly night came, and the moon appeared bloody, and in the skies I watched this severed head roll, wrapped in mourning.)

This is an extraordinary example of the gradual transformation of a landscape by an inner vision.

The invocation to the Muse of Indignation quoted earlier concludes with the word "epic," which is the key to the larger design of *Châtiments*; for the book is not just a collection of Juvenalian satires in the tradition of Régnier, Boileau, and other French imitators of the Romans, but like Agrippa d'Aubigné's *Tragiques*, the French work which it most resembles, there are attempts to go beyond the normally static quality of satire and gather the momentum of a huge vision of history. The satiric sections on a Juvenalian pattern alternate or are combined with passages inspired by the biblical prophetic model, in which the casting of anathema and cries of woe culminate in visions of a rightful order restored or a revelation. The *I* of the prophet is, of course, an almost impersonal, inspired one and not to be confused with the private *I* of much lyric poetry. It is in this way that we must understand the famous "Ultima verba" with its concluding line, *Et s'il n'en reste qu'un, je serai celui-là.* Much fun has been made of this line through lack of seeing it in the prophetic context. Early in *Châtiments* Hugo establishes the *I* who is but the instrument of God rather than an individual speaking to other individuals:

> *O Dieu vivant, mon Dieu! prêtez-moi votre force,*
> *Et, moi qui ne suis rien, j'entrerai chez ce Corse*
> *Et chez cet inhumain;*
> *Secouant mon vers sombre et plein de votre flamme,*
> *J'entrerai là, Seigneur, la justice dans l'âme*
> *Et le fouet à la main . . .*   ("A l'obéissance
> passive" ["To Passive Obedience"])

(O living God, my God! lend me your strength, and I who am nothing will enter the abode of the Corsican beast, brandishing my verse, dark and full of your flame; I will go in, Lord, with justice in my soul and a whip in my hand.)

The prophetic threats are often among the most striking passages:

> *Avenir! avenir! voici que tout s'écroule!*
> *Les pâles rois ont fui, la mer vient, le flot roule,*
> *Peuples! le clairon sonne aux quatre coins du ciel;*
> *Quelle fuite effrayante et sombre! les armées*
> *S'en vont dans la tempête en cendres enflammées,*
> *L'épouvante se lève;—Allons, dit l'éternel!*   ("Carte d'Europe"
> ["Map of Europe"])

(Future! future! now everything is crumbling! The pale kings have fled, the sea comes, the wave rolls. Peoples, the trumpet blows at the sky's four corners. What a terrible and dark flight! Armies vanish in the storm like burning ashes; terror is rising. "Come," says the eternal!)

> *Pendant que dans l'auberge ils trinquent à grand bruit,*
> *Dehors, par un chemin qui se perd dans la nuit,*
> *Hâtant son lourd cheval dont le pas se rapproche,*
> *Muet, pensif avec des ordres dans sa poche,*
> *Sous ce ciel noir qui doit redevenir ciel bleu,*
> *Arrive l'avenir, le gendarme de Dieu.*   ("On loge à la nuit"
> ["A Night's Lodgings"])

(While they noisily drink toasts in the inn, outside, by a path which vanishes into the night, hurrying his heavy horse, whose step draws near, silent, thoughtful, with orders in his pocket, under the black sky which will be blue again, there arrives the future, God's police.)

The static quality of traditional satire which foresees no change is thus altered by this admixture of the prophetic mode and its vision of the future.

The prophetic voice implies a design which is to be fulfilled, and Hugo tried to infuse his volume with historical myth. The famous "L'Expiation" ("The Expiation") placed near the center of *Châtiments,* deals with Napoleon I, his fall, and the crime, his own coup d'état, which led to it. The Second Empire, headed by Napoléon le petit, is at once the parody of the first one and the penance undergone by the shade of the great Emperor. Making myth out of recent history is not an easy undertaking, and I do not feel that "L'Expiation" is an adequate poem, attempting as it does to impose on events still in living memory a providential pattern in which few could believe. Disbelief, of course, can be suspended, in the famous phrase, but only when artistry prevails over it, and "L'Expiation" is perhaps too long-winded and explicit to convey even fleetingly the illusion Hugo sought.

The division of *Châtiments* into sections, most of them titled by a Rightist cliché (for example, "L'Ordre est rétabli" ["Order is Reestablished"]), is more a matter of convenience in breaking up the volume rather than a question of design. The real principle behind the arrangement of the poems in the first five books is variety in length, tone, and verse form. There are pieces of a distinctly jocular nature as well as lurid ones, song forms beside alexandrine couplets or quatrains. However, as we draw near the last book ("Les Sauveurs se sauveront" ["The Saviors Will Save Their Skins"]), and the concluding poem "Lux," which balances the introductory "Nox," evocations of nature can be found, notably in "Stella":

> *Un ineffable amour emplissait l'étendue.*
> *L'herbe verte à mes pieds frissonnait éperdue. . .*
> . . . .
> *J'entendis une voix qui venait de l'étoile*
> *Et qui disait:—Je suis l'astre qui vient d'abord.*
> *Je suis celle qu'on croit dans la tombe et qui sort.*
> *J'ai lui sur le Sina, j'ai lui sur le Taygète.*
> *Je suis le caillou d'or et de feu que Dieu jette,*
> *Comme avec une fronde, au front noir de la nuit.*

(An indescribable love filled the expanses; the grass at my feet quivered ecstatically. . . I heard a voice coming from the star and saying, "I am the star who comes first. I am the one they think is in the grave and who has come back. I shone on Mount Sinai, I shone on Mount Taygetus; I am the pebble of gold and fire which God casts, as if with a slingshot, against the night's black brow.")

The star is the forerunner (notice the reference to Elijah) of the Angel Liberty, and the apocalyptic note is unmistakable and appropriate. Historically, apocalypse grew out of the later prophets' style of utterance, and Hugo's myth concludes, like the Bible's, with a symbolic vision. The use of symbols is especially striking in poems like "Sonnez, sonnez toujours . . ." ("Blow, Still Blow"), which deals with the battle of Jericho, "Le Chasseur noir" ("The Black Huntsman"), in which the Wild Huntsman of Germanic legend is transformed into an avenger, and "L'Egout de Rome" ("The Sewer of Rome"), the culmination of all the references to decadent Rome which run throughout *Châtiments*. "Lux" draws on many biblical sources, and especially the voice from the whirlwind in Job:

> Qui donc a traversé l'espace,
> La terre, l'eau, l'air et le feu,
> Et l'étendue où l'esprit passe?
> Qui donc peut dire: "J'ai vu Dieu!
>
> . . . .
>
> "J'ai vu cette main inconnue,
> "Qui lâche en s'ouvrant l'âpre hiver,
> "Et les tonnerres dans la nue,
> "Et les tempêtes sur la mer,
>
> "Tendre et ployer la nuit livide;
> "Mettre une âme dans l'embryon;
> "Appuyer dans l'ombre du vide
> "Le pôle du septentrion . . ."

(Who then has crossed space, land, water, air, and fire, and the reaches where spirit can pass? Who then can say: "I have seen God!. . . I have seen that unknown hand which, when it opens, can release bitter winter and bolts of thunder in the dark cloud and storms upon the sea? I have seen it stretch out and fasten down leaden night, place a soul in the embryo, anchor, in the shadow of nothingness, the northern pole.)

The inspiration for these lines lies in such passages as the following:

Where wast thou when I laid the foundations of the earth? declare if thou hast understanding. . . . Who shut up the sea with doors, when it brake forth, as if it had issued out of the womb? When I made the cloud the garment thereof, and thick darkness a swaddling band for it. . . . Hast thou perceived the breadth of the earth? declare if thou knowest it all. . . . Who hath divided a watercourse for the overflowing of waters, or a way for the lightning of thunder? (Job 38:4, 8, 9, 18, 25)

The passage from "Lux" is far from the most powerful and original use of Jobian rhetoric, with its sarcastic questions and grandiose themes, that we shall find in Hugo's later work. Here he remains rather close to his model in types of imagery. Later, as we shall see, the basic rhetorical framework and tone of God's voice in Job will be combined with striking new images of Hugo's invention but in keeping with the spirit of the biblical book.

The Jobian passage in "Lux" now yields to a more affirmative tone and the vision of a great tree, the Edenic tree of life, which has become identified with progress. And thus the cycle of history closes on a note which for some readers may seem discordantly secular, given the biblical analogies that precede, but which is characteristic of a whole strain of non-Christian yet religious epic literature of the French Romantic period.[1] Visions of social redemption seemed for many Romantics, in fact, more in accordance with the notion of deity than the Christian concept of personal salvation. As it will shortly become clear, Hugo elaborated a theology to support his apocalyptics.

II   *"La Vision de Dante"*

The link of inspiration of the major works of the 1850's is readily shown by the case of "La Vision de Dante" ("Dante's Vision"). Conceived of originally as forming a whole section of *Châtiments,* where it certainly would not have been out of place, the poem was removed from that volume and was not published until 1883 in the *Série complémentaire* of *La Légende des siècles.* (It is only one of many poems of the 1850's whose publication was postponed considerably for one reason or another.) The subject of "La Vision de Dante" consists of an attack on Pius IX, pope at the time of Hugo's imbroglio with Louis Napoleon and exile. The relative audacity of the piece—God assigns Pius IX to a place in hell—was probably the reason for its excision from *Châtiments.* What interests us about it, however, is the formal structure which is that of a prophetic-apocalyptic vision more closely patterned on biblical models than anything Hugo had written theretofore. The framework of biblical visions consists often of a series of figures or symbolic objects which appear to the poet as he falls into a kind of trance, and are sometimes accompanied by glosses. In Hugo's poem the vision is double: First Dante appears to him and speaks; the vision proper is Dante's, as he wakes from death in 1853. Amidst swirling chaos he sights two portals:

> *Alors je distinguai deux portes de nuées,*
> *L'une au fond, devant moi, l'autre en bas, au-dessous*
> *D'un brouillard composé des éléments dissous,*
> *Comme un puits qu'on verrait dans les eaux. La première,*
> *Splendide, semblait faite avec de la lumière;*
> *C'était un trou de feu dans un nuage d'or;*
> *Quelqu'un, celui qui parle aux sibylles d'Endor,*
> *Pour construire cet arc, splendide météore,*
> *Avait pris et courbé les rayons de l'aurore. . .*

(Then I saw clearly two gates in the clouds, one at a distance before me, the other low down, beneath a fog made of dissolving elements, like a well perceived in the midst of waters. The first one, dazzling, seemed made of light; it was a hole of fire in a cloud of gold. Someone, He who speaks to the sybils in Endor, had taken and bent the beams of dawn to build this arc, a shining meteor.)

This is the gate of heaven; the other will, of course, be that of hell. What is significant is that no further mention of the gates is made; they are there solely to indicate the genre in which Hugo is writing; we realize immediately it is that of the prophets. The procession of figures which follows, after an angel blows his trumpet, is that of victims of power in ascending order: martyrs, soldiers, captains, princes, and finally the source of evil power itself, the Pope, who is sentenced by God. This first experiment in what one might call formal vision sets an important precedent in Hugo's work; *Dieu*, which is cast in the same pattern, is perhaps a more beautiful, certainly a richer poem, but its form grows out of this earlier working out of the prophetic model.

III   *The Seances*

Between the writing of "La Vision de Dante" in February, 1853, and the publication of *Châtiments* in November of the same year, a peculiar and most significant event occurred in the life of Hugo and his entourage. Wife, children, and mistress had eventually followed him into exile and gathered about him first in Jersey and later in Guernsey, which he chose among the Channel Islands because, while British in sovereignty, they were more or less French speaking (Hugo never learned any other languages than decent Latin and faulty Spanish). The event was the arrival for a visit of a French friend, who introduced the Hugo household to table-rapping seances, which had become something of a fashion in Paris. The method used was the usual one, in which two or three people lay their hands on a table surmounted by a smaller one and wait for the little table to move or be struck by the spiritual forces at work. A conventional alphabet is then established in which so many raps indicate a certain letter, and communication can then begin. The participants in the room—they need not be at the table— ask their questions aloud and wait for a reply. The first seances were failures, but then suddenly contact was made, and the first spirit to speak was the dead daughter Léopoldine. The effect this created can be imagined. Hugo, who had been skeptical about the powers of the table, immediately grew interested, and, after some experimentation, it was discovered that the only powerful medium in the group was his son Charles, for whom the table would be positively loquacious. Soon the spirits of Shakespeare, Molière, and other famous dead, as well as abstractions like Death itself, began to manifest themselves. The communications were sometimes in verse and in the style of Hugo himself: It was clearly his un-unconscious that was being projected through his rather passive elder son, whose whole life was overshadowed and made difficult by the towering figure of his father. It was never even necessary for Hugo to be in the room, much less at the table, where he proved to be a worthless medium, for his preoccupations and mannerisms to embody themselves in the spirits. The whole family circle, however, was so steeped in his work and thought that they seemed never to notice this peculiarity, doubtless because at least two or three of them tended automatically to pastiche Hugo in their own work, as if his style were a universal one.

Although the seances were abandoned after a fit of madness on the part of one of the participants, the transcript of them was carefully preserved for posterity, and it is clear that, despite much empty verbiage and despite Hugo's refusal to take anything from the spirits verbatim for his own work, the shades served to encourage him in certain directions and to confirm much that was in his conscious mind. The whole episode has more than a merely anecdotal interest; the history and publication of some of Hugo's most important work may have been influenced by the seances.

IV *La Fin de Satan*

Although Hugo wrote many poems on religious themes in the 1830's, they contain no dogmatic theology; in fact, they hardly suggest that he had more than a quite vague, intuitive notion of God, not very different from that of Lamartine or other Romantics. With the concluding "Lux" of *Châtiments* and even more so with the last judgment scene of "La Vision de Dante," Hugo's poetry becomes a vehicle of eschatology, the doctrine of final things or the end of the world as we know it. Eschatological myths presuppose a theology of a certain elaborateness, rather than mere faith in God's goodness; they assume some vision of origins, some consideration of the divine attributes, and other concerns in the theological domain. Within a short time after *Châtiments* was published and perhaps before the revelations of the table had had their effect, Hugo began a long poem of great scope in its account of terrestrial history and divine design: *Satan pardonné (Satan Pardoned)*, or *La Fin de Satan*, as it came later to be called.

While Hugo was not the first or sole poet to conceive of such a theme, [2] his working out of it, though the poem remains incomplete, makes it peculiarly his own. Essentially, the poem was to consist of four sections "Hors de la terre" ("Beyond the Earth"), in which the drama of God and Satan would be enacted, and three intercalated episodes illustrating the cycle of evil on the earth: Nimrod the warrior's attempt to conquer heaven, the crucifixion of Christ, and the French Revolution. The four extraterrestrial sections are mostly finished; the French Revolution one was never written beyond a few lines. The gospel episode and some of the Satan passages were added in 1859 or 1860 when Hugo went back to his interrupted epic.

Hugo was, of course, attempting to rival Milton in his description of Satan's fall with which the poem opens, and the comparison is instructive. Whereas Milton organized his fallen angels into an orderly government set up in a visually conceivable nether world, Hugo's Satan falls alone through thousands of years in a strange chaos in which the only fixed points are the suns which die out one by one. Finally, as he breathes at the last sun hoping to make it burn brighter,

A ce souffle, un grand bruit troubla l'ombre, océan
Qu'aucun être n'habite et qu'aucuns feux n'éclairent,
Les monts qui se trouvaient près de là s'envolèrent,
Le chaos monstrueux plein d'effroi se leva
Et se mit à hurler: Jéhovah! Jéhovah!
L'infini s'entr'ouvrit, fendu comme une toile,
Mais rien ne remua dans la lugubre étoile;
Et le damné, criant:—Ne t'éteins pas! j'irai!
J'arriverai!—reprit son vol désespéré.
Et les glaciers mêlés aux nuits qui leur ressemblent
Se renversaient ainsi que des bêtes qui tremblent,
Et les noirs tourbillons et les gouffres hideux
Se courbaient éperdus, pendant qu'au-dessus d'eux
Volant vers l'astre ainsi qu'une flèche à la cible,
Passait, fauve et hagard, ce suppliant terrible.   ("Et Nox facta est")

(At this gust of breath a great noise stirred up the shadow, an ocean which
no being inhabits and no torches light up; the nearby mountains flew away;
monstrous chaos full of dread rose and began to howl, "Jehovah, Jehovah!"
Infinity half opened, split like a sheet, but nothing moved in the mournful
sun. The damned one, crying, "Don't go out, I'll go on, I am coming!"
set out again on his desperate flight. And the glaciers, mingling with the
nights which resemble them, turned upside down like trembling beasts,
and the black whirlwinds and the hideous chasms bent wildly, while above
them, flying toward the sun like an arrow to its target, there passed, wild and
haggard, that terrible supplicant.)

The spatial imagery is characteristic of the extraterrestrial
passages in *La Fin de Satan*. The verbs indicating motion form
no coherent picture, any more than do the nouns which are their
subjects. Even the direction of Satan's flight cannot be described
as up or down: Almost total spatial uncertainty prevails. The same
ambiguity is true of the animate and inanimate, between which no
clear line can be drawn. Hugo also works the sense of certain words
like *fauve* (and elsewhere *vermeil, azur, noir)* so that they have
special connotations in his verse and cannot always be taken
literally. Instead of projecting on his hell the familiar visual concepts
like above and beneath, as Milton does, Hugo creates a purely
verbal world which cannot be compared to the one we know except
in respect to light: Satan's hell is complete when the last sun is
extinguished; no medieval fire and brimstone enliven the landscape.
    Another significant difference between the traditional myth of
paradise lost and Hugo's is found in the account of the earth and

its creation. The pre-Adamites, the race of monsters which God destroyed, are alluded to at the end of "Et Nox facta est," the passage on Satan's fall. The first picture of earth is the Flood coming to destroy an evil creation whose deity is Lilith. Isis-Lilith, as Hugo identifies her, is Satan's daughter and Adam's first wife before Eve in esoteric tradition. All this parabiblical material is meant to suggest that the world began in evil, not in an idyllic garden. In other words, the cycle of fall and redemption begins with Lucifer's fall, not mankind's, for man is dependent on the creation and whatever evil it implies. After the Flood Lilith rises up with a nail, stick, and stone, the instruments with which Cain killed Abel. God could destroy man and beast, she affirms, but not matter. These three weapons in the form of a sword (Nimrod), a cross (the crucifixion), and a prison (the Bastille during the Revolution) provide the unifying element of the terrestrial episodes.

The second episode "Hors de la terre" deals with a feather from Lucifer's wings which did not fall with him and which is transformed into the Angel Liberty. This second daughter of Satan, so to speak, has been made to derive from the Cabalistic tradition according to which God has a female counterpart, Matrona, balancing Lilith's relation with Satan.[3] The notion is intriguing, but we should remember that L'Ange Liberté was already present in "Stella" in Châtiments. The need for symmetry could have determined the Angel Liberty episode, as well as esoteric lore.

"Le Gibet" ("The Cross"), the account of the crucifixion, need not detain us long. Gospel episodes mingle with invented ones, and there is a certain ambiguity about the presentation of Jesus, who was not a redeemer for Hugo, but nevertheless a holy figure. In any case, the point is made that Christ changed nothing in the moral scheme of things. The following extraterrestrial section, "Satan dans la nuit" ("Satan in the Night"), is, on the other hand, the pivotal point in the cycle of creation, fall, and redemption. "Je l'aime," Satan declares at the beginning, and what comes after is a long development, in a highly imagistic style, on his damnation. The old Christian definition of evil as the absence of good is the basis for Hugo's figurative language; *L'enfer, c'est l'absence éternel; Etre maudit, c'est là le bitume et le soufre.* At first Satan felt absence of light as a positive thing:

Oh! quand je fus jeté
Du haut de la splendeur dans cette cécité,

> *Après l'écroulement de l'ombre sur ma tête,*
> *Après la chute, nu, précipité du faîte*
> *A jamais, à la tombe inexorable uni,*
> *Quand je me trouvai seul au bas de l'infini,*
> *J'eus un moment si noir que je me mis à rire;*
> *La vaste obscurité m'emplit de son délire,*
> *Je sentis dans mon coeur, où mourait Dieu détruit,*
> *La plénitude étrange et fauve de la nuit...*

(Oh! when I was thrown from the height of radiance into this blackness, after shadow collapsed onto my head, after the fall, naked, cast from the summit forever, joined to the inexorable grave, when I found myself alone at the bottom of infinity, I had one moment so dark I began to laugh. Vast darkness filled me with its delirious joy; I felt in my heart, where God, undone, expired, the strange and wild fullness of night.)

We see how the imagery of dying suns encountered in "Et Nox facta est" has a genuine theological value, God being literally light. The "fullness" of darkness has yielded, however, to the realization of deprivation, *privatio boni,* in the classic Augustinian phrase:

> *Jadis, ce jour levant, cette lueur candide,*
> *C'était moi. — Moi! — J'étais l'archange au front splendide,*
> *La prunelle de feu de l'azur rayonnant,*
> *Dorant le ciel, la vie et l'homme; maintenant*
> *Je suis l'astre hideux qui blanchit l'ossuaire.*
> *Je portais le flambeau, je traîne le suaire;*
> *J'arrive avec la nuit dans ma main; et partout*
> *Où je vais, surgissant derrière moi, debout,*
> *L'hydre immense de l'ombre ouvre ses ailes noires.*

(Once the rising light, the white glow was I! I was the archangel with the gleaming brow, the eye of fire in the shining blue, making heaven, life, and man golden; now I am the hideous star whitening the bone yard. I bore the torch; I drag the winding sheet. I come with night in my hand, and, everywhere I go, looming up behind me, erect, the immense hydra of darkness opens its black wings.)

The vocabulary of dark and light is something more than a mere metaphoric equivalence of evil and good: Literal and figurative senses are inextricably bound together. Hugo's theological concepts are never wholly abstract; this is especially apparent as Satan arrives at the philosophical crux of his monologue. Light and shadow are again the terms in which the argument presents itself:

Oui, c'est l'énigme, ô nuit, de tes millions d'yeux:
Le grand souffrant fait face au grand mystérieux.
Grâce, ô Dieu! Pour toi-même il faut que je l'obtienne.
Ma perpétuité fait ombre sur la tienne.
Devant ton oeil flambeau rien ne doit demeurer,
Tout doit changer, vieillir et se transfigurer.
Toi seul es. Devant toi tout doit avoir un âge.
Et c'est pour ta splendeur un importun nuage
Qu'on voie un spectre assis au fond de ton ciel bleu,
Et l'éternel Satan devant l'éternel Dieu!

(Yes, it is the enigma, O night, of your millions of eyes: The great sufferer faces the great mysterious one. Forgiveness, O God, for Yourself I must have it. My eternalness casts a shadow on Yours. Before Your torch eye nothing should remain; everything should change, grow old, and become transformed. You alone are. Before You everything should have an age. That a specter can be seen seated in the depths of Your blue heavens is a cloud which flaws Your radiance: eternal Satan facing eternal God.)

The allusion here is to the dualism which Hugo found in Christian thought. "And the devil that deceived them was cast into the lake of fire and brimstone . . . and shall be tormented for ever and ever" (Revelations 20:10). A concept of creation in which there was a permanent place of evil repelled Hugo on moral and logical grounds. It is as if darkness had the power to actively withstand light. This is demonstrated in the conclusion to "Hors de la terre" III, where the Angel Liberty advances toward Lilith, who simply disappears at the approach of light. Satan, meanwhile, has fallen asleep, the conclusion to another theme of "Satan dans la nuit": Not only is hell absence of light and love, but absence of sleep and rest, as Satan hears ceaselessly the evil he cannot see from his dark abode.

After the few fragments of the French Revolution episode comes a short final, doubtless incomplete, section in which Satan is reunited with God. Here the theology of radiance shows peculiarities which we must explore at least briefly:

Oh! l'essence de Dieu, c'est d'aimer. L'homme croit
Que Dieu n'est comme lui qu'une âme, et qu'il s'isole
De l'univers, poussière immense qui s'envole;
Mais moi, l'ennemi triste et l'envieux moqueur,
Je le sais, Dieu n'est pas une âme, c'est un coeur.
Dieu, centre aimant du monde, à ses fibres divines
Rattache tous les fils de toutes les racines,

> *Et sa tendresse égale un ver au séraphin;*
> *Et c'est l'étonnement des espaces sans fin*
> *Que ce coeur, blasphémé sur terre par les prêtres,*
> *Ait autant de rayons que l'univers a d'êtres.*

(Oh! the essence of God is loving. Man believes that God is only a soul like himself and that He has withdrawn from the universe like an immense cloud of dust vanishing. But I, the sad enemy and envious mocker, I know God is not a soul, He is a heart. God, the loving center of the world, attaches to His divine fibers all the rootlets of all roots, and His tenderness is the same for seraph and worm, and it is the amazement of the endless expanses that this heart, blasphemed on earth by priests, has as many beams as the universe has beings.)

The refutation of the idea that God is a soul seems to mean that no personal relation with deity exists, that the latter cannot be separated from the creation. God as a heart is a pantheistic conception according to which godhead is immanent and a force much like gravity or magnetism. The implications are that the cycle of creation, fall, and reunion with deity is essentially an impersonal process represented by the mythic Satan and in which man plays a somewhat passive role. There are no covenants, elect souls, or chosen tribes as in the Bible. While this interpretation may misrepresent somewhat the complexity of Hugo's religious thought, it shows a clear direction in which his theology was tending and which was shortly to be made even more explicit.

V "Ce que dit la bouche d'ombre"

La Fin de Satan occupied Hugo during the spring of 1854, and, when he ceased work on it, it was to devote himself to lyric poems, often on religious themes, which were to be published in *Les Contemplations*, a work whose composition Hugo was growing more and more concerned with. Toward October of the same year, he finished another genuinely theological poem, "Ce que dit la bouche d'ombre" ("What the Mouth of Shadow Says"), which has a unique place in his work, not so much because of its beauty as because of the fullness with which his conception of deity and creation is set forth. Much that is implied or briefly alluded to in *La Fin de Satan* (such as images of weight) becomes clear in its intention in "Bouche d'ombre." The origins of Hugo's thought in the poem are somewhat mysterious. Prose notes dating from August, 1852, set out much of

the essential of the poem.[4] On the other hand, in the transcriptions
of the Jersey seances there is a passage in which Hugo at once claims
the matter of his poem to be a concern of long standing and admits
that the seances have played a role in its elaboration. Hugo addressed
the table on September 19, 1854, roughly about the time "Bouche
d'ombre" was written. Here are his words:

I have a serious question to ask. The beings who inhabit the invisible . . .
know that for about twenty-five years I have been preoccupied with the
questions the table brings up and delves into. . . .In this labor of twenty-five
years I had arrived at several of the results which are contained today in
the table's revelation. . . . I was for a moment annoyed in my wretched
human vanity by the revelation. . . . The being called Idea . . . has *ordered*
me to write verse on the captive, punished beings which make up, for the
uninitiate, inanimate nature. I obeyed. I had to go into detail, a degree
of detail which contains my previous thought along with the breadth
contributed by the new revelation.[5]

If we take the table's revelation as springing from Hugo's unconscious desires, then we may, of course, still look for the sources
of it in his reading or experience. But first we must look at some of
the crucial passages near the beginning of the poem.

A specter appears to the poet at the opening, in a reminiscence
of Daniel 14:35, and then upbraids him in the Jobian manner. The
prophetic time and place are established carefully according to
biblical tradition. The actual revelation begins only with lines 54 on:

> *Dieu n'a créé que l'être impondérable.*
> *Il le fit radieux, beau, candide, adorable,*
> *Mais imparfait; sans quoi, sur la même hauteur,*
> *La créature étant égale au créateur,*
> *Cette perfection, dans l'infini perdue,*
> *Se serait avec Dieu mêlée et confondue,*
> *Et la création, à force de clarté,*
> *En lui serait rentrée et n'aurait pas été.*
> *La création sainte où rêve le prophète,*
> *Pour être, ô profondeur! devait être imparfaite.*
>
> *Donc, Dieu fit l'univers, l'univers fit le mal.*
> . . . .
>   *Or, la première faute*
> *Fut le premier poids.*
>   *Dieu sentit une douleur.*
> . . . .
> *Le mal, c'est la matière. Arbre noir, fatal fruit.*

(God created only unweighable being. He made it radiant, beautiful, shining white, worthy of worship, but imperfect; otherwise, being on the same plane, the created equal to the creator, such perfection, lost in infinity, would have mingled and merged with God, and creation, because of its great brilliance, would have returned into Him and would not have existed. Holy creation, of which the prophet dreams, in order to be, O mystery, had to be imperfect. Thus, God made the universe; the universe made evil. . . . Now then, the first transgression was the first weight. God felt a pang of pain. . . . Evil is matter, black tree, deadly fruit.)

The debate over the sources of this theology has gone on for many years.[6] It has been argued that the idea of the imperfection of creation and the evilness of matter are commonplaces from the Church Fathers on.[7] On the other hand, the author of one of the earliest, most fascinating, and most attacked studies of Hugo's religion, Denis Saurat, maintained, seemingly with good reason, that the spatial conception of God, Who was omnipresent, separating Himself from creation or retreating from part of Himself in order to allow creation to exist, which would seem to be implied in the above lines, is an esoteric doctrine to be found originally in the Zohar, the thirteenth-century distillation of the Jewish Cabala.[8] Saurat supports his contention by tracing Hugo's relations with an Alsatian Jew, Alexandre Weill, who published more or less Cabalistic works.[9] But does Hugo's notion that God first made being, which then created evil, actually represent Cabalism? Why should Hugo refer to something that sounds like original sin (*la première faute*)? The following passage seems to insist on a kind of personal transgression in keeping with Christianity:

> *Ne réfléchis-tu pas lorsque tu vois ton ombre?*
> *Cette forme de toi, rampante, horrible, sombre,*
> *Qui, liée à tes pas comme un spectre vivant,*
> *Va tantôt en arrière et tantôt en avant,*
> *Qui se mêle à la nuit, sa grande soeur funeste,*
> *Et qui contre le jour, noire et dure, proteste,*
> *D'où vient-elle? De toi, de ta chair, du limon*
> *Dont l'esprit se revêt en devenant démon;*
> *De ce corps qui, créé par ta faute première,*
> *Ayant rejeté Dieu, résiste à la lumière;*
> *De la matière, hélas! de ton iniquité.*
> *Cette ombre dit:—Je suis l'être d'infirmité;*
> *Je suis tombé déjà; je puis tomber encore.—*
> *L'ange laisse passer à travers lui l'aurore;*

> *Nul simulacre obscur ne suit l'être aromal;*
> *Homme, tout ce qui fait de l'ombre a fait le mal.*

(Do you not reflect when you see your shadow? Whence comes this form of you, crawling, horrible, somber, which, bound to your steps like a living specter, goes sometimes ahead and sometimes behind, which mingles with night, its great fatal sister, and which, hard and black, protests against light? It comes from you, from your flesh, from the mire your spirit clothes itself with as it becomes a demon; from the body, which, created by your first sin, having rejected God, resists light; from the matter, alas, of your evildoing. The shadow says, "I am frail being; I have already fallen; I can fall still more." Dawn can pass through the angels; no dark image follows an aromal being. Man, whatever casts a shadow has done evil.)

Provisionally we cannot absolutely distinguish Hugo's theology from Christianity, but, as the poem unfolds, the differences will become clear.

The idea of the Great Chain of Being is next introduced and presented as moving from God down to pure matter such as stones; it takes an especially striking form as the nadir of creation is described: *Un affreux soleil noir d'où rayonne la nuit.* At first we may think of a dualistic vision of the universe, but Hugo is slowly developing his thought.

"God does not judge us," the specter announces as the central exposition begins. Men are free to rise or fall along the Chain of Being; evil men descend into things: *L'âme du noir Judas depuis dix-huit cents ans,/Se disperse et renaît dans les crachats des hommes.* Beasts and stones are prisons for souls, where they contemplate God and their separation from Him. Their expiation contrasts with man's oblivion of his earlier incarnations (metempsychosis is an essential part of Hugo's design), and the possibility of approaching godhead is his. He is blind, unlike beasts and stones, but free. He occupies the middle realm between that of the angels and that of fatality-stricken lower beings. All this material has analogues in ancient and modern esoteric thought: The sources are so numerous as to discourage any attempt to posit the particular influence of this or that writer on Hugo. The important thing to note, however, is the process of justice Hugo describes. It is a system in which God does not intervene. This, as we saw in *La Fin de Satan,* is the distinctive feature of much occultist or esoteric thought: It envisions a far more *rational* scheme of things than Christianity, a less anthropomorphic notion of deity. The attraction occultism had in the nineteenth century lies unquestionably in the fact that it is a reasonable, logical alternative to Christianity; it rejects flagrantly primitive myths and replaces them with a quasi-scientific process of creation and evolution. Despite the ambiguous earlier passages on the first *faute*, Hugo's deity is emphatically not in the Christian tradition. *Oui, ton fauve univers est le forçat de Dieu*, exclaims the specter, giving us an important key to some of the nature imagery we encounter not only in "Bouche d'ombre" but elsewhere. A demonic vision of the universe is quite in keeping with the conception of a world-prison, "God's convict." To take one example, the normal connotations of flowers are reversed: *Tous ces sombres cachots qu'on appelle les fleurs* ("Bouche d'ombre," v. 685). Yet by a dialectic shift the world becomes an object of pity as much as of horror, since beast, stone, and object are engaged in expiation. Therefore hope can exist, and nature can be seen as evolving upward. Hugo abruptly shifts from alexandrine couplets to lyric stanzas for the final section of "Bouche d'ombre," and in passages reminiscent of parts of "Satan dans la nuit" redemption is seen:

> *On verra le troupeau des hydres formidables*
> *Sortir, monter du fond des brumes insondables*
> *Et se transfigurer;*
> *Des étoiles éclore aux trous noirs de leurs crânes,*
> *Dieu juste! et, par degrés devenant diaphanes,*
> *Les monstres s'azurer!*

(It will be that the dreadful hydras' herd will come forth, rise from the depths of unfathomable fog and be transformed; stars will flower in their skull's black holes, just God! and becoming gradually diaphanous, monsters will fade into the blue.)

At the end Christ is united with Belial in a reworking of the idea of *La Fin de Satan*. The anti-Christian character of this is emphasized by the choice of the name Belial rather than Satan for the fallen angel; Hugo is contradicting Saint Paul's implication in II Corinthians 6:14–15: "What communion hath light with darkness? And what concord hath Christ with Belial?"[10] The dualism of Christianity has been superseded.

There are several sometimes lengthy poems written or finished shortly before or after "Bouche d'ombre" and closely related to it; they develop above all its notions of punishment and redemption, rather than its cosmogony, for in the latter respect "Bouche d'ombre" is unique in Hugo's work. Of these poems, "Pleurs dans la nuit" ("Tears in the Night"), "Horror," "Dolor," and "Magnitudo parvi" found a place in *Les Contemplations;* publication of others was postponed perhaps because of their close resemblance to parts of "Bouche d'ombre." They are all of high poetic quality, however, and "Tout le passé et tout l'avenir" ("The Whole Past and Future") and "Inferi," which appeared in the second and third series of *La Légende des siècles* (1877 and 1883) respectively, deserve particular mention. But the most extraordinary—and lengthy—theological poem Hugo was to write after "Bouche d'ombre" was the "Solitudines coeli," "Dieu," or "L'Océan d'en haut" ("The Ocean Above") section of *Dieu,* which occupied him in the early months of 1855.[11]

VI   Dieu *("L'Océan d'en haut")*

At the table-rapping seances in 1855, the shades were still confirming Hugo in his beliefs. On March 8, the notion of redemption contained in *La Fin de Satan,* which had been begun, according to a note of Hugo's, precisely one year before, was expounded by a spirit.[12] Later in the month Christ manifested Himself and described the new religion that would replace Christianity in terms that are somewhat hazy, but in which we can recognize themes of the last sections of "L'Océan d'en haut." Hugo asked if Christ knew his recent work and received a negative response.[13] The first clear information about the poem is contained in the journal of Hugo's daughter Adèle.

Night of May 1–2. . . . My father read his poem on religions and began by speaking of the religion of Siva—then of the religion of Good and Evil—struggle between Good and Evil—it was midnight—my father wearily folded his manuscript saying that two hours of poetry ought to be enough. Everyone protested. . . . He continued; he spoke of Judaism; finally he got to the religion of Christ; it was one o'clock. . . . My father spoke of the revelations of the seances; then he finally got to his own religion which can be summarized in the one great word Love. . . . It was 2:30 A.M. . . .M. Aug[uste Vacquerie, Hugo's principal disciple] thinks it very fine that after his own religion my father announced another one at the end of the poem and thus left the door of the future open.[14]

Adèle Hugo's description of what was then called "Solitudines coeli" is accurate in its suggestion of the scope and ambitiousness

of Hugo's poem. It is constructed on a form of the prophetic pattern
we have already seen: The poet finds himself in a strange spot where
symbolic creatures appear and speak. The first four visions, those
of a bat, a crow, and, in a later addition, an owl and a vulture,
present the viewpoints of atheism, doubt, dualism, and polytheism;
all are filled with striking examples of Hugo's demonic imagery.
The bat, for example, who represents Hugo's own peculiar interpretation of Sivaism as godlessness, unfolds a sinister vision of the
Great Chain of Being we have encountered in "Bouche d'ombre":

> *Toute gueule est un gouffre, et qui mange assassine.*
> *L'animal a sa griffe et l'arbre a sa racine;*
> *Et la racine affreuse et pareille aux serpents*
> *Fait dans l'obscurité de sombres guets-apens.*
> *Tout se tient et s'embrasse et s'étreint pour se mordre;*
> *Un crime universel et monstrueux est l'ordre...*

(Every maw is a chasm and he who eats murders. The animal has its claw
and the tree its root, and the root, horrible and snakelike, sets dark ambushes
in the night. All things cling together and hug and embrace to bite each other.
Universal, monstrous crime is the order of the world.)

The chain is not one of rising moral qualities, but rather a closed
infernal circle; the interdependence of the links comes from mutual
destructiveness.

The owl's speech contains an equally somber vision of the
universe:

> *Les morts et les vivants, qui sont une vapeur,*
> *Se mêlent; le volcan, crête et bouche enflammée,*
> *Vomit un long siphon de cendre et de fumée;*
> *L'air se tord, sans qu'on sache où l'aquilon conduit*
> *Les miasmes pervers et traîtres de la nuit;*
> *La marée, immuable et hurlante bascule,*
> *Balance l'océan dans l'affreux crépuscule;*
> *Et la création n'est qu'un noir tremblement.*
> *On ne sait quelle vie émeut lugubrement*
> *L'homme, l'esquif, le mât, l'onde, l'écueil, le havre;*
> *Et la lune répand sa lueur de cadavre.*

(The dead and the living, who are a vapor, mingle. The volcano, a fiery
crest and mouth, vomits a long spout of ashes and smoke. The air writhes,
without anyone's knowing where the north wind takes the perverse,
treacherous miasmas of night. The tide, an unchanging, screaming seesaw,
rocks the ocean in the dread twilight. And creation is only a black trembling.

No one knows what life mournfully informs man, skiff, mast, wave, reef, harbor; and the moon casts its cadaverous glow.)

In much of *Dieu* God's presence, qualities, or absence is indicated by visions of nature; Hugo's theology is never abstract but argues the creator from the creation, so that magnificent visions of the universe fill the poem.

This passage also illustrates some characteristic prosodic and syntactic structures of Hugo's later verse. The sentence structure is often simplified into parallel, paratactic constructions, such as we find in much biblical poetry; the striving for complex and varied sentence patterns, at which we have seen Hugo excel in his earlier poetry, still persists, but alternates with this new reduction of syntax to basic elements. The latter would seem awkward in a lesser poet, but Hugo chose it to give his images their fullest impact; there is a driving quality about repetition which only a poet of his skill could exploit for all its worth. Enumeration, as in the tenth line above, is another form that parallelism of simple grammatical elements often takes. The possible monotony of such syntax is carefully counterbalanced by a freedom in handling the alexandrine couplet which is rarer in his earlier work, save for the plays, where the so-called *alexandrin brisé* was considered acceptable. Enjambment, often combined with strong stops other than at the caesura (as in line two above), alternates with the sentence-verse line or sentence-couplet to produce variety. And finally, the internal structure of the alexandrine has been modified radically. Hugo is famous for the 4/4/4 division of the alexandrine in his later work, but there are other tripartite patterns to be found which are generally considered much rarer and more the property of Verlaine and Mallarmé. For example, lines five, six, and eleven above lend themselves more readily to the divisions 3/5/4, 3/6/3, and 3/6/3 than to the traditional patterns.

The third vision of "L'Océan d'en haut" consists of the crow's speech, which represents, under the guise of Zoroastrianism, a kind of lopsided Manichean dualism. The speech takes the form of a short myth or prophecy, in which Ahriman, the force of darkness, overcomes Ormazd, the god of light. We should point out that the various sections of "L'Océan d'en haut" do not present a historically accurate or chronologically sequential account of religions, but are rather a series of theological propositions arranged in order of increasing complexity. Thus the two gods of Part Three precede the vision of polytheistic paganism in the vulture's speech. The latter presents nature as a teeming mass of copulating forces: Prostitution and the sexuality of an evil female dominant deity presiding over lesser ones are its major themes. Hugo's break with the conventional poetic representation of classical deities, which is generally perceptible in his work, reaches one of its most original expressions here.

As we might expect, the eagle who represents (for uncertain reasons) Judaism delivers a speech in Jobian rhetoric, proclaiming the nothingness of man before God and the dangers of divine wrath. Out of the multiple aspects of Christian theology, Hugo chose to emphasize, in the griffon's speech, which constitutes the sixth vision, clemency and forgiveness, which counterbalance original sin. However, he does not fail to remind us that hell is eternal for those who die unshriven or at least unrepentent. The angel who speaks next represents the revelation of the seances, as Adèle Hugo put it, or rationalism, as one editor accurately, if unjustifiably, entitled this section. This consists essentially of the same material we found in "Bouche d'ombre," less the cosmogony. Eternal damnation and anthropomorphic attributes of deity are refuted as a prelude to expounding the notion of the universe as being in eternal moral progress.

In the final section of "L'Océan d'en haut," as the poem existed in 1855, the poet-prophet sees a brilliant light approach, which delivers a speech that in its pantheistic character resembles some parts of the angel's discourse (Hugo did not always handle theology with minute care for distinctions), but consists more of ejaculations such as "la nuit n'est pas" than an argument. Its high point is a vision of godhead as light:

> *Rien n'existe que lui, le flamboiement profond,*
> *Et les âmes,—les grains de lumière, les mythes,*
> *Les moi mystérieux, atomes sans limites,*
> *Qui vont vers le grand moi, leur centre et leur aimant;—*
> *Points touchant au zénith par le rayonnement,*
> *Ainsi qu'un vêtement subissant la matière,*
> *Traversant tour à tour dans l'étendue entière*
> *La formule de chair propre à chaque milieu;*
> *Ici la sève, ici le sang, ici le feu;*
> *Blocs, arbres, griffes, dents, fronts pensants, auréoles,*

Retournant aux cercueils comme à des alvéoles;
Mourant pour s'épurer, tombant pour s'élever,
Sans fin, ne se perdant que pour se retrouver,
Chaîne d'êtres qu'en haut l'échelle d'or réclame,
Vers l'éternel foyer volant de flamme en flamme...

(Nothing exists but Him, the deep flaming, and souls—the specks of light, myths, mysterious *I*'s, limitless atoms, which move toward the great *I*, their center and magnet—points touching the zenith with their beams, tolerating matter like a garment, passing through the formula of flesh suitable to each level, one at a time, in the whole of space: here sap or blood or fire; blocks, trees, claws, teeth, pensive brows, haloes, returning to the coffin as to a honeycomb cell, dying to be purified, falling to rise, endlessly, being lost in order to be found, the chain of beings that the golden ladder above summons, flying from flame to flame toward the eternal source.)

The Great Chain of Being is here, as in "Bouche d'ombre," but the "ancient metaphysics of light," as Denis Saurat put it, is far more in evidence than in the earlier poem. Matter is simply ignored or denied existence. It is as if, looking down from the top of the chain, the poet could perceive nothing but the brilliance surrounding him. *Dieu n'a qu'un front: Lumière! et n'a qu'un nom: Amour!* is the concluding line of the speech, and in the last word we find not so much the indication of a relation with God, for we are all part of deity, as a theology which is at once mystical and impersonal.

VII   Dieu *("Le Seuil du gouffre")*

As we mentioned earlier, Hugo had had the idea of a volume to be called *Les Contemplations* at least since 1852. His conception of the work gradually evolved in the next four years, which were also a period when he produced large quantities of verse of the most varied inspiration, as well as the philosophical and visionary works we have been considering. Although *Les Contemplations* is often referred to as Hugo's major collection of lyric poetry, the work is much more than that. It is a spiritual autobiography, but almost an impersonal one. "Ah! fool, to think I am not you," Hugo addresses the reader in the preface. Accordingly, the earlier books ("Autrefois") contain poems suggestive of youth, and even bear false dates or dates which are not necessarily those of the poem's composition, but of a period in Hugo's life he wishes to evoke: The autobiographical element is often stylized rather than literal. At times, distinctly personal experiences intrude, as at the beginning of the second half ("Aujourd'hui") with poems on the death of Léopoldine, Hugo's daughter. Toward the end the work becomes more and more philosophical as mournful poems written in exile occur, as well as hints of Hugo's theology. (Attempts to determine a more complex "architecture" in *Les Contemplations* seem to me forced and futile.) The ending of the volume was naturally a crucial problem; Léopoldine's death dominated the second half to a certain degree, but elegy was not what Hugo wanted, except for the splendid "A celle qui est restée en France" ("To Her Who Remained in France"), which forms a kind of epilogue. Hugo's experience with table-rapping convinced him that death was merely part of a larger process, and so the work had to achieve a larger philosophical viewpoint. He had the choice between two great visionary conclusions: "Ce que dit la bouche d'ombre," and "L'Océan d'en haut." With some prodding by friends, he chose the former, which was shorter, less likely to unbalance the structure of the volume, and might be inconspicuous enough not to fuel excessively the inevitable hostile reviews. This decision left Hugo with his most lengthy and ambitious poem still in manuscript. Hugo's natural urge to modify (usually by amplification) his poems or collections of poems right up to publication time went to work, and as *Les Contemplations* was appearing in 1856, he was busy expanding "L'Océan d'en haut" into a longer work and writing a new complementary poem, "Le Seuil du gouffre" ("The Threshold of the Abyss").

This new part of *Dieu* was again a visionary poem derived in its framework from the Bible. A strange beast appears before the poet, identifies itself as *L'Esprit humain,* and then a series of voices issue from the creature, each one developing the theme that God is unknowable. The rhetoric is sometimes Jobian, the imagery always demonic. The God-seeker is often identified as a *mage,* which brings up an interesting point. One of the long poems toward the end of *Les Contemplations* is called "Les Mages" ("The Magi"), and in it a great many poets and thinkers are enumerated as belonging to the elite of true priests or leaders of humanity, which is the special sense the word *mage* acquires for Hugo. But in "Le Seuil du gouffre" the *mage* meets with a strange fate:

Qui que tu sois, redoute, au gouffre où tu te plonges,
Le vague coudoiement des vains passants des songes.

. . . .

Ce n'est pas sans danger que des hommes d'argile,
Tremblants quand ils sont las, glacés quand ils sont nus,
Dialoguent dans l'ombre avec des inconnus.   ("Voix III" ["Voice III"])

(Whoever you are, dread, in the chasm into which you are plunging, the wandering contact of the empty fleeting spirits of dreams. . . . Not without danger do men of clay, trembling when they are tired, chilled when they are naked, speak in the shadow with unknown ones.)

Godhead is described as an abyss, the sinister counterpart of deity's being on high. Once in the depths, the *mage* is exposed to losing direction and being tossed about as if weightless:

Un souffle vous apporte, un souffle vous remmène.
On a, sur ce qu'on garde encor de forme humaine,
D'obscurs attouchements et des passages froids;
Toute l'ombre n'est plus qu'une suite d'effrois;
On sent les longs frissons des roseaux de l'abîme.

(A puff brings you closer, a puff takes you back. You are, on whatever is left of your human form, darkly touched and coldly brushed. The whole shadow now is but a series of terrors. You feel the long shivering of the reeds of the abyss.)

The imagery is not unlike that of "Et Nox facta est" in *La Fin de Satan.* Here two grammatical devices typical of Hugo's visionary poetry are employed to render the eerie abyss which cannot quite be visualized: The verb is reduced to a neutral, colorless one, as in *on a,* but coupled with a verbal noun such as *attouchements* or *passages.* These verbal nouns are furthermore in the plural, which makes them even more elusive and unsusceptible of visual rendering. The pluralizing of abstract nouns like *effrois,* on the other hand, gives them a half concrete sense: individual things producing fright. The hypallage or transfer of sense in *frissons* (it is the *mage* who shudders at the contact with the reeds, which themselves would appear to be trembling) is also characteristic of Hugo's mature rhetoric.

The verb is further reduced a few lines later to a mere infinitive:

Etre de la clameur dans l'infini semée,
Un vague tourbillon pleurant, une fumée

De larves, de regards, de masques, de rumeurs,
De voix ne pouvant pas même dire: je meurs,
Passant toujours, toujours, toujours, comme un flot sombre,
Sous les arches sans fin du hideux pont de l'ombre!

(To be clamor sown in infinity, a wandering, weeping whirlwind, a smoke of masks, glances, grimaces, rumblings, of voices incapable of even saying, "I am dying," passing forever like a dark wave under the endless arches of the shadow's hideous bridge.)

The play between abstract and concrete meanings is again noticeable here, but what is perhaps most striking is the image which concludes the voice's speech. Nothing is more characteristic of Hugo's visionary imagery than geometric or architectural forms (circle, spiral, staircase, tower, wall, bridge, arch, portico). These motifs, which we saw as early as "Puits de l'Inde. . ." in *Les Rayons et les Ombres,* find their greatest expressivity in the demonic apocalyptic mode of Hugo's later poetry.

The relation of "Le Seuil du gouffre" to the earlier "L'Océan d'en haut" is not entirely clear. Editors have printed it as a prologue to the original poem, but there seems to be evidence that Hugo thought of it as a conclusion.[15] At the same time as he wrote "Le Seuil du gouffre," he added a new and brief final section to "L'Océan d'en haut" called "Le Jour" ("Day"), in which a shroud appears before the poet, touches him, and he dies. The *mage,* in short, is vanquished in his search for God. Certainly "Le Seuil du gouffre" is among the most somber poetry Hugo ever wrote, and if it was to follow "L'Océan d'en haut," *Dieu* would be an expression of the most extreme despair and dejection. This is by no means out of keeping with Hugo's imagination, for, if his theology was adamantly melioristic and opposed to the supposed dualism of Christianity, his penchant for the demonic is undeniable and perhaps increased in his later years, as two of his novels and the supplements to *La Légende des siècles* would seem to show. Of course, the impression of dualism one tends to receive from his *oeuvre* as a whole does not run completely counter to the theology of "Bouche d'ombre" in the sense that the point of view taken, whether we look up or down the Great Chain of Being, will determine the color of our vision. But more important for a writer, perhaps, is the success with which he conveys his picture of the world, and it is true that for many readers Hugo's greatest success lay in depicting that shadow which is the absence of God, as Claudel put it.

"Le Seuil du gouffre" was never put into any final form, and the fact that Hugo never completed or published *Dieu* is one of the more mysterious problems in describing his career as a poet. The spirit of Death, with whom he spoke about "Bouche d'ombre" at a seance in September, 1854, answered one of his questions by saying that a great mind produces two *oeuvres,* his living one and his ghostly or posthumous one. It is possible that Hugo, who did indeed leave a sizeable amount of unpublished verse at his death, felt that he was obeying some occult plan in not releasing *Dieu* to the public. He did, on the other hand, eventually publish two works which are closely related to *Dieu,* one of them *L'Ane,* being almost contemporary with "Le Seuil du gouffre." *L'Ane,* begun perhaps in 1856, worked on in 1857–58, but not brought out until 1880, is a long critique of human thought addressed by a donkey to Kant. The rhetoric is often Jobian, the long lists of famous and obscure names and works similar to many passages in *Dieu.* The very conception of the poem situates it in the same climate of sarcasm and disparagement found in the greater work.[16] The other poem that is related in its themes and texture to *Dieu* is *Religions et Religion,* which contains some material from the 1850's, was largely written in 1870, and was published in 1880. The title alone is suggestive of the review of religious attitudes and ideas in *Dieu;* the form, however, is not in the prophetic tradition, although there are voices in it as in "Le Seuil du gouffre." An attack on both materialism and established religions, often Jobian in character, is its main burden. The style unfortunately does not rise to the heights Hugo was capable of; it is expert in its unified texture and masterly versification, but a certain monotony comes from the failure to achieve such brilliant climaxes as before.

The later history of *La Fin de Satan* also contains some peculiarities. In 1860, when he had finished the first series of *La Légende des siècles* and was very much in the habit of writing narrative poems, Hugo turned back to his first epic and filled it out with the gospel episode "Le Gibet" and some of the "Hors de la terre" passages, notably the ones on the Angel Liberty. The poem was still in a somewhat fluid state in his mind, however, as is attested by his intention at one point of including in it *La Pitié suprême.* This long poem was composed in 1857 and develops a theme of "Bouche d'ombre," that tyrants and other criminals are their own first victims and deserve pity. This could clearly have been a prelude to the redemption of Satan, but circumstances dictated otherwise, and *La Pitié suprême* was published by itself in 1878. *La Fin de Satan* thus remained in the schematic and incomplete form we know. Along with that of *Dieu,* Hugo referred to its future publication in the preface to *La Légende des siècles,* as if to force the hand of his publisher, who was reluctant to bring out overtly metaphysical poems, but practical considerations won out, and Hugo made his later reputation with the more popular genres of short narrative poetry, diatribe, lyric, and the novel.

CHAPTER 6

La Légende des siècles

I *Introduction*

THE idea of a volume of *petites épopées* ("little epics") had occurred to Hugo early in the 1850's, and examples of them date from even before, but it was not until the end of the greatest period of apocalyptic poetry in 1856 that he devoted himself primarily to that project. (From then also dates his increasingly flexible notion of epic.) His publisher was enthusiastic about the possibility of more exoteric poetry than *Dieu* or *La Fin de Satan*, and Hugo was able to finish the work, now called *La Légende des siècles*, in time for publication in 1859. It thus belongs, at least in part, to the period of incredibly abundant production in the decade following his exile—in part, not only because of earlier pieces, but above all because of the later additions to the work. A *Deuxième Série* of *La Légende* was published in 1877, a *Série complémentaire* in 1883. In the latter year, the three parts of *La Légende* were integrated into one another and brought out as a collective edition. The date of the last two parts does not, it should be said immediately, indicate anything about the dates of the poems contained in them; there are many pieces from the 1850's, some from the 1860's, and again a goodly number from the early 1870's, when Hugo had a great renewal of poetic inspiration.

The problems of studying *La Légende* as a composed or structured work derive from the vagaries of publication and a seemingly changing conception of what it was to represent. Taking legend in its ordinary sense, the 1859 form might seem best to conform to the title. The later additions seem at times quite remotely related to Hugo's original purpose. The role of Hugo's literary advisers is not to be underestimated, either, in the preparation of the collective *Légende*. On the other hand, if we confine our attention to the 1859 series, we would omit many important poems, some of which are contemporaneous with the pieces of that series. It seems best to compromise and take as our text the 1883 collective edition, skipping over whatever seems irrelevant. We shall have occasion to distinguish, in the course of our discussion, between the original core of *La Légende* and later accretions, whenever such a distinction seems advisable.

II The Early Centuries

Excluding the prefatory poem, to which we shall come back later, *La Légende* opens with evocations of biblical times. Our first impression is that the vision of the universe presented in *La Fin de Satan* has been abandoned. The first poem, "Le Sacre de la femme" ("The Crowning of Woman"), consists largely of a description of Eden. The point of that poem, that Eve first feels a child moving in her womb, is, besides being dramatically effective, a deliberate criticism of the 1854 Papal Bull on the Immaculate Conception, which outraged Hugo, for whom sensuality in nature and in divinity was a natural assumption.[1] The notion of man's fall is displaced onto Cain in "La Conscience" ("Conscience"), which ties in with the role of Cain's weapons in *La Fin de Satan*: Though the opening of *La Légende* seems rather conventional, its details are carefully thought out on nonorthodox lines. The poem devoted to cosmogony, "Puissance égale bonté" ("Power is Goodness"), is a stylized version of an Oriental myth. God and Eblis, the Islamic devil, vie in creating. All Eblis can make is a grasshopper. He gives God, as raw material for the latter's creation, a spider:

> *Et Dieu prit l'araignée et la mit au milieu*
> *Du gouffre qui n'était pas encor le ciel bleu;*
> *Et l'Esprit regarda la bête; sa prunelle,*
> *Formidable, versait la lueur éternelle;*
> *Le monstre, si petit qu'il semblait un point noir,*
> *Grossit alors, et fut soudain énorme à voir;*
> *Et Dieu le regardait de son regard tranquille;*
> *Une aube étrange erra sur cette forme vile;*
> *L'affreux ventre devint un globe lumineux;*
> *Et les pattes, changeant en sphères d'or leurs noeuds,*
> *S'allongèrent dans l'ombre en grands rayons de flamme;*
> *Iblis leva les yeux, et tout à coup l'infâme,*
> *Ébloui, se courba sous l'abîme vermeil;*
> *Car Dieu, de l'araignée, avait fait le soleil.*

(And God took the spider and put it in the middle of the abyss, which was not yet the blue sky. And Spirit gazed at the creature. His terrible eye cast forth eternal light. The monster, so little it seemed a black dot, then grew larger and was suddenly enormous to look at. And God gazed at it with His quiet expression. A strange dawn shimmered over the vile shape. The horrid belly became a shining orb. And the legs, their articulations changing into golden spheres, stretched out into the shadow like great streaks of fire. Eblis looked upward, and suddenly the Unspeakable One, dazzled, crumpled over beneath the shining abyss. For God, out of the spider, had made the sun.)

Hugo has deliberately chosen to avoid at this point in *La Légende* any suggestion of sinister creation, such as we found in *La Fin de Satan*. The reason is one of tone: He wishes to keep serious metaphysics out of the beginning of the work, so that the biblical poems will seem serene, even to some extent the one dealing with Cain, in contrast to the later deepening of evil. "Puissance égale bonté" is interesting in that the spider, which we have seen as early as *Notre-Dame de Paris*, and which occurs frequently in Hugo's demonic imagery, is converted to good by the same process of metamorphosis we have seen at the end of "Ce que dit la bouche d'ombre." Here, however, the emphasis is on the brilliance of the image, not on a theological conception.

To the symbolism of godhead as sun and staring eye (in Cain's tomb for example—this representation of God has many antecedents as does the notion, common in ancient science, that eyes cast light) Hugo joins that of withdrawal, of invisibility in "Dieu invisible au philosophe" ("God Invisible to Philosophers") and "Suprématie" ("Supremacy"), an Indian legend of competition among gods. The latter poem is one of several later additions to *La Légende* which develop the theme of God's power over inferior deities, suggested in "Puissance égale bonté." The struggle between the Olympians and the Titans provides the subject of several poems, of which the most beautiful perhaps is "Le Titan." In it Phtos, one of the conquered race of giants, crawls through the earth, in which he is imprisoned, and emerges on the other side:

> Il sent en lui la joie obscure de l'abîme;
> Il subit, accablé de soleils et de cieux,
> L'inexprimable horreur des lieux prodigieux.
> Il regarde, éperdu, le vrai, ce précipice.
> Evidence sans borne, ou fatale, ou propice!
> O stupeur! il finit par distinguer, au fond
> De ce gouffre où le jour avec la nuit se fond,

A travers l'épaisseur d'une brume éternelle,
Dans on ne sait quelle ombre énorme, une prunelle!

(He felt in himself the dark joy of the abyss. Overwhelmed by suns and skies, he was subject to the inexpressible horror of these fantastic places. Frantically he looked at the chasm of truth. Endless proof, either deadly or favorable! O amazement! he finally sighted, in the depths of this abyss, where day mingles with night, through the density of an eternal mist, in some enormous shadow, a staring eye.)

To the Olympians Phtos then announces the reign of a superior god. It is not hard to see that the Titan poem, as well as "Suprématie," where God vanishes to prove his surpassing powers, is closely related to all the theological and visionary poems we looked at in the previous chapter. This is the most characteristic kind of addition Hugo made to the first *Légende*: These poems represent a continuation of his immediately preceding vein of apocalypse.

One general remark should be made about the poems of *La Légende*: They could be variously classified as descriptive ("Le Sacre de la femme"), anecdotal ("Dieu invisible au philosophe"), epigrammatic ("Le Temple"), short narrative ("La Conscience"), apocalyptic ("Le Titan"), or even lyric (the famous "Booz endormi" ["Boaz Asleep"], which is structured by an image pattern rather than the narrative, which is implicit). Hugo exploited to its fullest the vague character of the word legend, which is not so precise as epic, myth, heroic poem, or lyric evocation of the past, all of which are included in it. The original conception of *petites épopées* did not designate merely epic as it is ordinarily understood. The scope and ambition of *La Légende* justifies calling it epic, but of course in formal terms we should have to say that it is a nineteenth-century replacement for epic. The old epic conventions had not functioned adequately since Milton's time, although poets still felt the need of some kind of work which would claim to account for the destiny of mankind.

III *Medieval Times*

After the poems on biblical themes and the conflict between the gods, we encounter, amidst a good deal of apocalyptic material added in the later series, a large group of poems on medieval subjects. The notion of power, here translated into political terms, connects them with such pieces as "Le Titan." These are more narrative in the conventional way than the preceding groups; they also reveal, better perhaps than any others, certain basic patterns in Hugo's imagination. One might expect poems on medieval subjects to partake of the conventions of romance: birth of hero, struggle, winning of wife, and monumental death. We rarely find, however, any suggestion of romance as the Middle Ages understood it, or as Romantic poets like Keats or Tennyson tried to recreate it. Especially lacking is the nostalgia for a great vanished age, such as we find in the *Idylls of the King* or "The Eve of Saint Agnes." Instead, we are given somber dramas of brutality and retribution, bloody accounts of tyrants and kings. Against this background stand out the figures of the protector and protégé, as it has been put.[2] The former is often a knight, the latter an orphan. The protector is an extension of God's power, and, to complete the triangle, there is a source of evil power, such as a ruler or relative. Mountains, towers, and forests constitute the characteristic setting.[3] Some of the dramatic qualities of these narratives can be seen, for example, in the end of "La Confiance du marquis Fabrice" ("The Marquis Fabrizio's Trustfulness"), where, after Ratbert has murdered the orphaned heiress and her grandfather, his own head is mysteriously severed:

> *Le glaive qui frappa ne fut point aperçu;*
> *D'où vint ce sombre coup, personne ne l'a su;*
> *Seulement, ce soir-là, bêchant pour se distraire,*
> *Héraclius le Chauve, abbé de Joug-Dieu, frère*
> *D'Acceptus, archevêque et primat de Lyon,*
> *Etant aux champs avec le diacre Pollion,*
> *Vit, dans les profondeurs par les vents remuées,*
> *Un archange essuyer son épée aux nuées.*

(The sword that struck was not seen; no one knows where this dark stroke came from. Except that, in the evening, spading to pass the time, Heraclius the Bald, abbot of Joug-Dieu, brother of Acceptus, archbishop and primate of Lyons, standing in the fields with the deacon Pollion, saw, in the depths of the sky roiled by the winds, an archangel wipe his sword on the clouds.)

In the pattern of revelation of a greater power, or retribution, the archangel replaces the grandfather. Elsewhere knights act without divine intervention, but the schematic narrative pattern remains and can even be found elsewhere than in the medieval narratives of *La Légende*, although it is in its greatest evidence there.

Hugo's narrative style in *La Légende* deserves some comment. There are frequent passages where what we might call the abyss imagery, familiar to us from *La Fin de Satan* and *Dieu*, heightens the texture; it is in keeping with the somber mood and hint of the supernatural characteristic of many poems. On the other hand, there is necessarily a good deal of straightforward narrative in which great metaphoric embellishment would be out of place and delay the action. Hugo frequently resorts to speeches to convey elements of plot, and in this way we see how *La Légende* can be considered to a certain extent the continuation of Hugo's dramatic penchant. (Certainly *Les Burgraves* has strong resemblances to the later poetic narratives.) At the same time, connective material between speeches must be handled efficiently but in such a way as not to distract from the style of the speeches. Here Hugo tends to use an evocative but relatively subdued diction, in which short sentences or sentence fragments are meant to render movement. From "Le Petit Roi de Galice" ("The Little King of Galicia"), here is Roland's battle against the evil *infantes*:

> *Et dans le même instant, entre les larges roches,*
> *A travers les sapins d'Ernula, frémissant*
> *De ce défi superbe et sombre, un contre cent,*
> *On pouvait voir encor, sous la nuit étoilée,*
> *Le groupe formidable au fond de la vallée.*
> *Le combat finissait; tous ces monts radieux*
> *Ou lugubres, jadis hantés des demi-dieux,*
> *S'éveillaient, étonnés, dans le blanc crépuscule,*
> *Et, regardant Roland, se souvenaient d'Hercule.*
> *Plus d'infants; neuf étaient tombés; un avait fui. . .*

(And at the same moment, between the broad rocks, through the pines of Ernula, quivering from the proud and dark challenge, "one against one hundred," there could still be seen, under the starry night, the formidable group in the bottom of the valley. The battle was ending; all the radiant or mournful mountains, once the haunt of demigods, were waking, astonished, in the white dawn light, and, looking at Roland, remembered Hercules. No more *infantes*; nine had fallen; one had fled.)

The personification of the mountains is not dwelt on at length; it is primarily a device to bring in the comparison with Hercules. The latter is just one of the many, many effects Hugo sought from names in *La Légende*. In the preceding quotation from "La Confiance du marquis Fabrice," picturesqueness is produced by proper nouns. Elsewhere, as here, it is an air of grandeur that Hugo is after. Hugo was a great student of reference works, especially Moreri, a seventeenth-century encyclopedic dictionary from which he derived quantities of information (and misinformation) to lend historical color to his narratives. It would not be an exaggeration to say that Hugo's conception of epic style was inseparable from the use of proper nouns. Certainly it does not lie in any archaizing linguistic nostalgia, such as tempted other Romantic poets.

IV *"Le Satyre"* and the Final Meaning of La Légende

The medieval (and Oriental) poems which form so characteristic a part of *La Légende* would seem to indicate some darkening in the cyclic balance between good and evil. In the center of the collection Hugo placed a pivotal poem, "Le Satyre," under the heading "Sixteenth Century—Renaissance—Paganism." The meaning Hugo wished to convey by these terms is somewhat paradoxical, since in it the Olympians (who are, after all, the major pagan gods), are overturned. As for the sixteenth century, it should be taken perhaps more as a symbolic time rather than as a real event in human history. "Le Satyre" is a poem rich in implications which exceed those of a single moment in the legend of the ages.

A picture of a satyr living on Mount Olympus and disturbing nature by his priapic inclinations sets a rather light, fablelike tone at the beginning of the poem. For having molested Psyche he is brought before the gods, who are merely amused by him and order him to sing. Critics persist in ascribing this opening to some unlikely influence of Offenbach's operettas, forgetting that, in translation, certain scenes among the gods in the *Iliad* (for example, the end of Book I) seem oddly jocular. Hugo's purpose, in any case, is to effect a transition from frivolity to solemnity, as the satyr's song begins. First the terror of nature is his subject:

> *Le satyre chanta la terre monstrueuse.*
> *L'eau perfide sur mer, dans les champs tortueuse,*
> *Sembla dans son prélude errer comme à travers*
> *Les sables, les graviers, l'herbe et les roseaux verts;*
> *Puis il dit l'Océan, typhon couvert de baves,*
> *Puis la Terre lugubre avec toutes ses caves,*
> *Son dessous effrayant, ses trous, ses entonnoirs,*
> *Où l'ombre se fait onde, où vont des fleuves noirs,*
> *Où le volcan, noyé sous d'affreux lacs, regrette*
> *La montagne, son casque, et le feu, son aigrette,*

> *Où l'on distingue, au fond des gouffres inouis,*
> *Les vieux enfers éteints des dieux évanouis.*

(The satyr sang of monstrous earth. Water, treacherous at sea, sly and twisting in the fields, seemed to wander through his prelude as through sand, pebbles, green grass and reeds. Then he told of the ocean, a giant Typhaeus covered with slaver, then earth, mournful with its caves, its terrifying underside, its holes, its funnels, where shadow becomes water; where black rivers flow; where the volcano, drowned under dread lakes, longs for the mountain, its helmet, and fire, its plume; where can be seen in the depths of unheard-of chasms the old burnt-out hells of vanished gods.)

We recognize the cosmogony of *La Fin de Satan* here and the demonic, downward-looking, subterranean vision of nature which occurs in *Dieu*. Familiar themes come back: April like a beast in heat, the world as a chaos of copulation and creatures devouring each other, or sinister dawn and monstrous trees:

> *Derrière le réseau ténébreux des vertiges,*
> *L'aube est pâle, et l'on voit se tordre les serpents*
> *Des branches sur l'aurore horribles et rampants. . .*

(Behind the shadowy network of vertigo, dawn is pale, and there can be seen, writhing against the sunrise, serpents of branches, horrible and crawling.)

> *O nature terrible! ô lien formidable*
> *Du bois qui pousse avec l'idéal contemplé!*
> *Bain de la déité dans le gouffre étoilé!*
> *Farouche nudité de la Diane sombre*
> *Qui, de loin regardée et vue à travers l'ombre,*
> *Fait croître au front des rocs les arbres monstrueux!*
> *O forêt!*

(O terrible nature! O terrible bond between the growing wood and the ideal vision! Deity's bath in the starry abyss! Wild nakedness of the dark Diana, who, spied from afar and through the shadows, makes monstrous trees grow on the brow of rocks! O forest!)

Suddenly the satyr begins to praise chaos from which all things necessarily come and which now is seen as the principle of fecundity. We have previously encountered in Hugo's poetry the kind of shift of perspective which changes evil into good, and this is one of the most interesting examples of it. After praise of nature comes the song of man and his fate:

Il chanta l'Homme. Il dit cette aventure sombre:
L'homme, le chiffre élu, tête auguste du nombre,
Effacé par sa faute, et, désastreux reflux,
Retombé dans la nuit de ce qu'on ne voit plus;
Il dit les premiers temps, le bonheur, l'Atlantide;
Comment le parfum pur devient miasme fétide...

(He sang of man. He told of that dark adventure: Man, the chosen cipher, the august chief of numbers, who was erased by his own fault, and, like a disastrous ebbing, fell back into the night in which nothing can be seen. He told of the first days, happiness, Atlantis, how the pure scent becomes a fetid vapor.)

In a now poisoned world men unite:

En vain, frères, ils ont tué la Haine infâme,
Le monstre à l'aile onglée, aux sept gueules de flamme;
Hélas! comme Cadmus, ils ont bravé le sort;
Ils ont semé les dents de la bête; il en sort
Des spectres tournoyant comme la feuille morte,
Qui combattent, l'épée à la main, et qu'emporte
L'évanouissement du vent mystérieux.
Ces spectres sont les rois; ces spectres sont les dieux.

(In vain, like brothers, they killed infamous hatred, the monster of the winged claw and seven maws of flame. Alas, like Cadmus, they defied fate. They sowed the beast's teeth, from which there arose specters whirling like the dead leaf, who do battle, sword in hand, and are borne off by the vanishing mysterious wind. These specters are kings; these specters are gods.)

Man's vain struggle is then followed by a prediction of his rise from matter and fatality to aerial being:

Qui sait si quelque jour, grandissant d'âge en âge,
Il ne jettera pas son dragon à la nage,
Et ne franchira pas les mers, la flamme au front!
Qui sait si quelque jour, brisant l'antique affront,
Il ne lui dira pas: "Envole-toi, matière!"
S'il ne franchira point la tonnante frontière...
. . . . .
Prends le rayon, saisis l'aube, usurpe le feu;
Torse ailé, front divin, monte au jour, monte au trône,
Et dans la sombre nuit jette les pieds du faune!

(Who knows whether some day, growing from age to age, he will not throw his dragon into the water and cross the seas with fire on his brow! Who

knows whether some day, ignoring the ancient indignity, he will not say,
"Fly off, matter," whether he will not cross the thundering boundary. . .
Take the sunbeam, seize the dawn, usurp fire. With a winged torso and divine
brow, rise to light, to the throne, and into somber night cast the faun's
feet.)

Along with themes we have found in the visionary works, there
are references to technology, veiled but precise. We begin to realize
that Hugo's faun is a complex symbol in that he partakes of both
nature and mankind; he is at once part of the lower order of beings
and the prophet of a new one. Suddenly he acquires one of Hugo's
attributes of godhead, the staring eye, as he predicts the end of the
Olympians:

> *Vous avez au-dessus de vous d'autres esprits,*
> *Qui, dans le feu, la nue, et l'onde et la bruine,*
> *Songent en attendant votre immense ruine.*
> *Mais qu'est-ce que cela me fait à moi qui suis*
> *La prunelle effarée au fond des vastes nuits!*

(You have above you other spirits, who, in fire, cloud, wave, and rain,
meditate as they await your immense destruction. But what is that to me,
who am the staring eye in the depths of the vast nights!)

The metamorphosis of the satyr into Pan, that is, "all," follows,
while the frightened Olympians are reduced to impotence:

> *Tout en parlant ainsi, le satyre devint*
> *Démesuré; plus grand d'abord que Polyphème,*
> *Puis plus grand que Typhon qui hurle et qui blasphème,*
> *Et qui heurte ses poings ainsi que des marteaux,*
> *Puis plus grand que Titan, puis plus grand que l'Athos;*
> *L'espace immense entra dans cette forme noire;*
> *Et, comme le marin voit croître un promontoire,*
> *Les dieux dressés voyaient grandir l'être effrayant;*
> *Sur son front blêmissait un étrange orient;*
> *Sa chevelure était une forêt; des ondes,*
> *Fleuves, lacs, ruisselaient de ses hanches profondes. . .*

(While speaking so, the satyr became huge, bigger to begin with than Poly-
phemus, then bigger than Typhaeus, who screams and blasphemes and
beats his fists like hammers, then bigger than Titan, than Mount Athos.
Immense space invaded his dark form, and, as the sailor sees a promontory
grow in size, the gods, erect, saw the frightening being become larger.
On his brow there glimmered a strange dawn. His hair was a forest; waves,
rivers, lakes streamed down his deep thighs.)

We find in "Le Satyre" a more complicated problem of interpretation than in the more discursive poems like "Ce que dit la bouche d'ombre," because its mode is symbolic. Pantheism is suggested by the ending, as well as the reconciliation of man and nature. But the Chain of Being, the elaborate scheme of justice and expiation have vanished. On the other hand, an allegorical gloss in terms of progress, of society's entering into a new phase, seems a valid if partial reading. The symbol of the faun, unlike Hugo's more obvious symbols, can be built on, transformed, and manipulated, so that its value is not constant, as in a simple allegory.[4] "Le Satyre" can be interpreted in various ways, putting the emphasis on false deities, social renewal, Promethean discoveries or whatever, because it fulfills the need of richness and even ambiguity proper to sophisticated symbolism. "Le Satyre," in short, has more the qualities of a myth than of an allegory.

If we place "Le Satyre" in the context of La Légende, one aspect of the work becomes clear: Mankind as a collectivity is represented in it, whereas earlier poems of the collection tend to deal with isolated individuals.[5] After "Le Satyre," various "modern" poems in La Légende deal with historical events in a way that suggests their involving of classes, peoples, or nations. While the modern poems tend not to seem especially epic in the way the earlier ones do, Hugo clearly had an element of design in mind when he found a place for them. However, the presence of apocalyptic poems among them adds a further note of disparity to the second half of La Légende.

The concluding poems of La Légende were originally "Pleine Mer" ("Out at Sea") and "Plein Ciel" ("Up in the Sky"), a vision of humanity rising airborne, and "La Trompette du jugement" ("The Judgment Trumpet"). The latter confirms the impression given by the opening Edenic "Sacre de la femme," that Hugo had in 1859 wanted to avoid expounding any esoteric theology in La Légende. He was, in other words, trying to find a relatively conventional pattern for his work. By the time of the final Légende, Hugo no longer had to be concerned with whether his books sold or were well received, and he was free to include more visionary material in the work. Aside from the many apocalyptic poems added in the course of filling out La Légende, the new opening and closing pieces, "La Vision d'où est sorti ce livre" ("The Vision from which this Book Came") and "Abîme" ("The Abyss") suggest the more somber side of Hugo's inspiration (they were both written in the 1850's but withheld). The prefatory poem contains one of Hugo's most vivid uses of architectural imagery:

> *Et qu'est-ce maintenant que ce livre, traduit*
> *Du passé, du tombeau, du gouffre et de la nuit?*
> *C'est la tradition tombée à la secousse*
> *Des révolutions que Dieu déchaîne et pousse;*
> *Ce qui demeure après que la terre a tremblé;*
> *Décombre où l'avenir, vague aurore, est mêlé;*
> *C'est la construction des hommes, la masure*
> *Des siècles, qu'emplit l'ombre et que l'idée azure,*
> *L'affreux charnier-palais en ruine, habité*
> *Par la mort et bâti par la fatalité...*

(And what now is this book, translated from the past, the grave, the abyss, and night? It is tradition fallen in the wake of the revolutions that God unleashes and propels, what remains after an earthquake, a wreck mingled with the vague dawn of the future. It is man's construction, the hovel of the ages, filled with shadow and made azure by thought; it is the dreadful charnel-house palace in ruins, inhabited by death and built by fate.)

The equation of buildings with time adds a dimension to these lines that earlier uses of fantastic architecture did not have, and the identification of the very building materials with fate enriches the latter notion. It is clear that Hugo's historical cycle was not one whose completion could be more than glimpsed, and in the concluding "Abîme" God declares, *Je n'aurais qu'à souffler et tout serait de l'ombre.* The symbols of God as sun, eye, and invisibility reach their climax here: The hidden God, whose power is expressed as much by darkness as by light, seems to have been meant by Hugo to summarize his notions of deity.

V Torquemada

La Légende des siècles grew in its final form to such proportions and included so bewilderingly varied an array of poems that it is difficult to pick out more than a few recurrent features in it. And there are poems in such collections as *Les Quatre Vents de l'esprit* and *Toute la Lyre* which would fit beautifully into its fabric. One work which deserves particular mention for the quality of some of its verse and which would not have been out of place in *La Légende* is the drama *Torquemada,* written in 1869 and published in 1882. Of the various plays Hugo wrote after 1850 and which he did not destine for production, *Torquemada* is unique in its somber brilliance.[6] Another dramatic piece, "Welf," found its way into *La Légende,* but *Torquemada* was probably too long for inclusion. Its genre, however, the historical drama, is closely related, as we have noted, to many pieces of *La Légende,* with their long speeches and stylistic similarities to Hugo's earlier plays at their best.

Torquemada is a story about the fifteenth-century Inquisitor General of Spain, who condemned thousands to be burnt at the stake for heresy. Hugo's play has him as an unknown monk, condemned to death by his bishop for his radical doctrines; escaping thanks to a young royal couple; rising, through the Pope's favor, to a position of supreme power in Spain, where he may exercise his theology of purification by fire. His fanaticism obliges him in the end to condemn the couple who originally saved him.

There is an atmosphere of overripe and perverted religiosity in the play which brings to mind Villiers de l'Isle-Adam and the Symbolists right from the beginning, where the bishop has Torquemada entombed alive. The pageantry of black- and white-robed penitents, hooded and bearing the banner of death, is operatically exploited, as is the fear and tension of Ferdinand and Isabella discovering that their absolute power has been undermined. The pope in *Torquemada* is the infamous Borgia one, Alexander VI, which adds another sinister note to the religious theme. This last consists of Torquemada's belief that autos-da-fé are acts of love to redeem souls in peril. His great speech on the subject is one of the high points of Hugo's dramatic art. The monologue takes place before the *quemadero* in which Jews and heretics burn:

> *Oh! j'ai pansé la plaie effrayante de l'ombre.*
> *Le paradis souffrait; le ciel avait au flanc*
> *Cet ulcère, l'enfer brûlant, l'enfer sanglant;*
> *J'ai posé sur l'enfer la flamme bienfaitrice,*
> *Et j'en vois, dans l'immense azur, la cicatrice.*
> . . . .
> *Plus d'enfer. C'est fini. Les douleurs sont taries.*
> . . . .
> *Feu! lavage*
> *De toutes les noirceurs par la flamme sauvage!*
> *Transfiguration suprême! acte de foi!*

Nous sommes deux sous l'oeil de Dieu, Satan et moi.
Deux porte-fourches. Lui, moi. Deux maîtres des flammes.
Lui perdant les humains, moi secourant les âmes;
Tous deux bourreaux, faisant par le même moyen
Lui l'enfer, moi le ciel, lui le mal, moi le bien;
Il est dans le cloaque et je suis dans le temple.
Et le noir tremblement de l'ombre nous contemple.
(Il se retourne vers les suppliciés.)
Ah! sans moi, vous étiez perdus, mes bien-aimés!
La piscine de feu vous épure enflammés.
Ah! vous me maudissez pour un instant qui passe,
Enfants! mais tout à l'heure, oui, vous me rendrez grâce...
....

Car les blancs seraphins, penchés au puits de soufre,
Raillent le monstrueux avortement du gouffre,
Car votre hurlement de haine arrive au jour,
Bégaie, et, stupéfait, s'achève en chant d'amour!

(Oh, I have bandaged the frightening wound of shadow. Paradise was
suffering. Heaven had in its side an ulcer, burning hell, bloody hell. I
placed on hell the beneficent flame, and in the great blue sky I see the scar
from it.... No more hell. It is over. Sorrows are quenched.... Fire!
laving all blackness with the wild flame! Supreme transfiguration! Act
of faith! We are two under the eye of God, Satan and I. Two fork-bearers,
he, I. Two masters of the fire. He destroying humans, I aiding souls. Both
executioners creating by the same means, he hell, I heaven, he evil, I good.
He is in the sewer while I am in the temple. And the black trembling shadows
contemplate us both. Ah! without me, you would have been lost, my
dearly beloved! The pool of fire purifies you in flames. Ah! you curse me
for a passing instant, children, but soon you will thank me.... For the
white seraphim, leaning over the brimstone pit, laugh at the undoing of
the abyss; for your screams of hate reach the light, stammer, and, dumbfounded, become a chant of love!)

Hugo's imagination for the demonic reaches a new peak here:
Torquemada is a satanic enemy of Satan, by a kind of fantastic
situation in which opposites are paradoxically the same. Torquemada even conceives of the end of evil and eternal damnation
in an infernal version of total salvation. This is one step beyond
the other representations of evil in Hugo and has an eerie dramatic
effect. As Swinburne put it,

But when Hugo brings before us the figure of the grand inquisitor in contemplation of the supreme act of faith accomplished in defiance of king and

queen to the greater glory of God, for the ultimate redemption of souls else condemned to everlasting torment, the rapture of the terrible redeemer, whose faith is in salvation by fire, is rendered into words of such magical and magnificent inspiration that the conscience of our fancy is wellnigh conquered and convinced and converted for the moment as we read.[7]

CHAPTER 7

The Later Lyrics

I *Introduction*

THE editor of the huge one-volume Pauvert edition of Hugo's *Oeuvres poétiques complètes*—which excludes the plays—states that it contains over one hundred fifty thousand lines of verse, eight thousand or so of which are to be found in the *reliquats*, a term Hugo used to designate poems or fragments originally intended for a specific volume and then rejected for various reasons. This gigantic corpus of verse was produced by a poet whose work habits were regular, almost as if he were not a Romantic believer in inspiration but a Neoclassical craftsman of meter and diction. During the exile especially, Hugo had, with great pleasure, risen at dawn in his room on the top floor of Hauteville House—the grand residence on Guernsey paid for by the sales of *Les Contemplations*—and proceeded to write, sometimes using nocturnal *trouvailles,* and, in any case, throughout the morning hours. After the exile was terminated by the Franco-Prussian War in 1870, and after his involvement with politics at the beginning of the Third Republic, Hugo went back to Guernsey for a time, so that these writing habits remained with him more or less until a stroke in 1878 put an end to his imaginative powers.

Given the enormous body of Hugo's verse, we should hardly expect to find it all of equal interest—even when its skill is undeniable. Nor can we easily classify it all into convenient categories, a task which Hugo himself had difficulty in doing. For example, the lyric and invective often mingle, as in *Châtiments* (this, of course, is true of the biblical prophets), or the narrative and philosophical, as in *La Fin de Satan* or *La Légende des siècles.*

We have seen that *Les Contemplations* and *La Légende des siècles,* especially in its final form, are heteroclite in content; we may now say a word about the other later collections, before focusing on specific kinds of poems. *Les Quatre Vents de l'esprit* (1881) contains four books: lyric, satiric, dramatic, and epic. A first form of it (including most of the lyric section) was readied for publication by 1870, and contains much work contemporaneous with the collections of the 1850's; Hugo then added to it in the early 1870's. In the meantime, a purely lyrical volume, rather light in character, *Les Chansons des rues et des bois,* had appeared in 1865 (the verse largely dates from 1859); a kind of modern pastoral is its unifying tone. *L'Année terrible* (1872), devoted to the Franco-Prussian War and the Commune, exemplifies again the mixture of invective and lyricism so natural to Hugo and complicated this time by his ambivalent feelings about the fall of the Empire-France, the defeat which marked the end of his exile, and the general ambiguity of patriotism versus politics. *L'Art d'être grand-père* (1877) contains essentially light verse about the poet's grandchildren. Of the posthumous volumes, the two of *Toute la lyre* (1888 and 1893) correspond to an idea of Hugo's which he had not worked out in detail: Various periods and genres of verse are represented. *Les Années funestes* (1898) consists of pieces parallel to *Châtiments* and was so titled by Hugo, whereas *Dernière Gerbe* (1902) is purely the creation of his literary executor. The volume of *Océan* and *Tas de pierres* (1942)—the titles are Hugo's—contains fragments from all periods.

Of the four genres Hugo distinguished in *Les Quatre Vents de l'esprit,* drama, epic, lyric, and satire can be separated to some extent, but it is far more useful, for our purposes, to make a distinction between philosophical or visionary poetry, narrative, and shorter poems in which satire may not be distinct from lyric. (The fact that Hugo used alexandrine couplets for all genres means that no mechanical difference of prosody occurs.) Even within this threefold division, such a poem as "Horror" in *Les Contemplations* presents the ambiguity of being lyric in character but deriving from Hugo's philosophical cogitations. Nevertheless, there is a body of poetry we can identify as lyric if only by such negative features as the absence of narration, of theological implications, or of the biblical, prophetic, and apocalyptic conventions, and to this side of Hugo's *oeuvre* we shall now turn our attention.

Although many lyric poems fall into patterns which are familiar —the poem based on an analogy between two things or the one terminating in an epigram or conceit—we have no general theory of the forms—a morphology—of lyric. There are unquestionably period differences between lyric forms such as might separate Renaissance and Romantic lyric, but here again we are faced with the difficulty, if not impossibility, of trying to establish a canon of forms. We can say, however, that in Hugo's later work there is a characteristic and gradual intensification of effect through to the last lines of a poem—an intensification which is also noticeable in many narratives of *La Légende,* but even more so in the corpus of poems we shall call lyric. This progressive intensification is, furthermore, probably the only worthwhile criterion for distinguishing the apocalyptic-visionary mode from poems in which we feel equal brilliance and tension, but without the building up of feeling toward the end of the poetic structure. The apocalyptic-visionary mode puts the poem at a high-pitched emotive level right from the beginning. In the examples I am going to give of Hugo's later lyric style, we do not have this reference to a conventional form: We do not know, by their opening lines, that they fall into such and such a category. They begin in a quiet, less formalized way.

II *Song*

The prototypical poem is one which reminds us of song: Its prosodic and syntactic structure bespeaks subservience to a melody, even if the latter does not exist. We do not normally associate Hugo's name with this kind of lyric in the way we do the English or German Romantics. Nonetheless, there are enough poems of this sort in his *oeuvre* that Swinburne, in his *Study of Victor Hugo,* was able to quote a goodly number and perhaps give the impression that they are more frequently encountered than they are. Here is one of them:

> *Chanson*
> *Il est un peu tard pour faire la belle,*
> *Reine marguerite; aux champs défleuris*
> *Bientôt vont souffler le givre et la grêle.*
> *—Passant, l'hiver vient, et je lui souris.*
>
> *Il est un peu tard pour faire la belle,*
> *Etoile du soir; les rayons taris*
> *Sont tous retournés à l'aube éternelle.*
> *—Passant, la nuit vient, et je lui souris.*
>
> *Il est un peu tard pour faire la belle,*
> *Mon âme; joyeuse en mes noirs débris,*
> *Tu m'éblouis, fière et rouvrant ton aile.*
> *—Passant, la mort vient, et je lui souris.*
> *(Les Quatre Vents de l'esprit, III, 30)*

(It is a bit late to preen, Queen Daisy; in flowerless fields soon frost and hail will blow. O wayfarer, winter comes and I smile at it. It is a bit late, evening star, to preen. The weakened beams have all returned to eternal dawn. O wayfarer, night comes and I smile at it. It is a bit late to preen, my soul. Joyous in my blackened ruins you dazzle me, when, proud, you open your wing. O wayfarer, death comes and I smile at it.)

The use of only two rhymes is a kind of constraint Hugo did not usually seek out, but which he was most capable of handling gracefully. The classical epitaph, which addresses itself to the passerby, imposes a lapidary style in keeping with the recurrent line, and the whole is an elegant example of gradation up to a climax: words denoting or implying light and darkness alternating carefully between concrete and literal meanings. Hugo could handle this kind of poem with mastery, but it did not overly preoccupy him.

III   An Associative Thematic Structure

Far more typical of Hugo's most intense lyric work is the discursive poem in alexandrine couplets, and we shall look at seven of them, dealing with the traditional lyric themes of religion, nature, the imagination, and death. (No love poem is included in our choice for discussion; for a man of such great amorous capacities, Hugo's love poetry is singularly routine.) The first is "Halte en marchant" ("A Stop on a Walk"), which closes the first book of *Les Contemplations*. It is a remarkable example of shifting style and meditative movement:

> Une brume couvrait l'horizon; maintenant
> Voici le clair midi qui surgit rayonnant;
> Le brouillard se dissout en perles sur les branches,
> Et brille, diamant, au collier des pervenches.
> Le vent souffle à travers les arbres sur les toits
> Du hameau noir cachant ses chaumes dans les bois,
> Et l'on voit tressaillir, épars dans les ramées,
> Le vague arrachement des tremblantes fumées . . .

(A fog covered the horizon. Now here is bright noon rising up radiant. The fog dissolves into beads on the branches and shines like a diamond in the necklace of the periwinkles. The wind blows through the trees on the roofs of the black hamlet, which hides its thatched roofs in the woods. And you can see, scattered in the boughs, the vague streaks of trembling smoke shudder.)

The opening is at once an example of straightforward description and great verbal refinement. The word *diamant* used without a comparative "like," the concise and elegantly literary *épars*, and the verbal noun *arrachement*, doubly rare in its meaning and form, all contribute to the impression of great skill in diction, without, for that, seeming out of place in this description of ordinary countryside. The poet stops to eat at a peasant's cottage, where another train of thought than the pastoral is set off by one ornament of the simple room: *Et moi, près du grand lit drapé de vieilles serges,/Pensif, je regardais un Christ battu de verges.* Christ flagellated is the point of departure for a meditation on martyrdom in the broadest sense; the poet's thought is generalized and reaches back to Dante, Socrates, Aeschylus, and others:

> *Toujours au même but le même sort ramène.*
> *Il est, au plus profond de notre histoire humaine,*
> *Une sorte de gouffre . . .*
> . . . . . . , ... , ...
> *Le genre humain pensif—c'est ainsi que nous sommes—*
> *Rêve ébloui devant l'abîme des grands hommes.*
> *Ils sont, telle est la loi des hauts destins penchant,*
> *Tes semblables, soleil! Leur gloire est leur couchant . . .*

(The same fate always leads back to the same end. There is, in the depths of human history, a kind of chasm. . . . The pensive human race—and that's what we are—dreams bedazzled before the abyss of great men. They are, such is the law of declining high destinies, your equals, Sun! Their glory is their setting.)

The abyss image is developed in conjuction with that of the setting sun. The three stages of the poetic meditation—the morning and noon walk, the thought of great men greater in their sunsetlike decline, and the final nighttime section—contain a progression which is all the more effective in that it is not overemphasized, and the same may be said for the gradual movement from description to figurative meditation to the final example:

> *Un de ceux qui liaient Jésus-Christ au poteau*
> *Et qui sur son dos nu jetaient un vil manteau,*
> *Arracha de ce front tranquille une poignée*
> *De cheveux qu'inondait la sueur résignée,*
> *Et dit: Je vais montrer à Caïphe cela!*
> *Et, crispant son poing noir, cet homme s'en alla.*

La nuit était venue et la rue était sombre ;
L'homme marchait ; soudain, il s'arrêta dans l'ombre.
Stupéfait, pâle, et comme en proie aux visions,
Frémissant ;—il avait dans la main des rayons.

(One of those who bound Jesus Christ to the stake, and who threw a lowly cloak over his bare back, tore a handful of hair, damp with resigned sweat, from his calm brow and said, "I'm going to show that to Caiaphas." And clenching his black fist the man went off. Night had come and the street was dark; the man was walking. Suddenly he stopped in the shadow: dumbfounded, pale, as if seized by visions, quivering—beams of light were in his hand.)

The thought of Christ recurs unexpectedly in the concluding passage, and the image of supernatural light contrasts with the preceding ones of noon and sunset. At the same time, the title "Halte en marchant" acquires a completely new meaning here, as the poet and the soldier are both shown as pausing in contemplation of martyrdom. The religious theme is especially characteristic of Hugo's handling of Christianity: The life of Jesus provided him with a multitude of analogies and images without representing more than the fate of any great man. The gospel was a poetic treasure trove rather than a source of faith.

IV   *An Analogy*

Other poems of Hugo's show the same care for luminous concluding images as "Halte en marchant," but employ different means of arriving there. A particularly good example of the handling of a lengthy analogy is "Pasteurs et Troupeaux" ("Shepherds and Flocks"). The poet describes a valley in the Jersey landscape and the shepherdess he meets there:

J'y recontre parfois sur la roche hideuse
Un doux être ; quinze ans, yeux bleus, pieds nus, gardeuse
De chèvres, habitant, au fond d'un ravin noir,
Un vieux chaume croulant qui s'étoile le soir . . .
. . . .
Ses agneaux, dans le pré plein de fleurs qui l'encense,
Bondissent, et chacun, au soleil s'empourprant,
Laisse aux buissons, à qui la bise le reprend,
Un peu de sa toison, comme un flocon d'écume.
Je passe ; enfant, troupeau, s'effacent dans la brume ;
Le crépuscule étend sur les longs sillons gris

Des ailes de fantôme et de chauve-souris;
J'entends encore au loin dans la plaine ouvrière
Chanter derrière moi la douce chevrière . . .

(Les Contemplations)

(I meet there sometimes on the monstrous rock a gentle being, fifteen years old, blue-eyed, barefoot, a goat and sheep keeper, who lives down in a dark ravine, in a crumbling old thatched hut that is star-studded at night. . . . Her lambs, in the meadow full of flowers that perfume her, leap about, and each one, when the setting sun glows red, leaves on the bushes, from which the breeze carries it off, a bit of its fleece like a speck of foam. I go on; child and herd vanish in the fog. Twilight extends over the long grey furrows its ghostly batlike wings. I still hear, in the distance behind me, the gentle goatherd singing in the workaday plain.)

Suddenly the sea is present; nothing up to now except the simile between fleece and foam has prepared us for this switch in setting:

Et, là-bas, devant moi, le vieux gardien pensif
De l'écume, du flot, de l'algue, du récif,
Et des vagues sans trève et sans fin remuées,
Le pâtre promontoire au chapeau de nuées,
S'accoude et rêve au bruit de tous les infinis,
Et, dans l'ascension des nuages bénis,
Regarde se lever la lune triomphale,
Pendant que l'ombre tremble, et que l'âpre rafale
Disperse à tous les vents avec son souffle amer
La laine des moutons sinistres de la mer.

(And down there, before me, the pensive old herder of foam, water, seaweed, reef, and waves relentlessly and endlessly moving, the shepherd-headland capped with clouds, leans on his elbow, dreaming in the noise of all infinity, and, in the elevation of blessed clouds, watches the triumphant moon rise, while the shadows tremble and the harsh gust casts to the wind with its bitter breath the wool of the sea's sinister sheep.)

The literal shepherdess and flock behind the poet is now a figurative one before him. This metaphoric shepherd-headland (a vivid example of the grammatical construction, rare in all writers save Hugo, by which nouns are juxtaposed to make an imagistic whole) contrasts, of course, with the shepherdess in age and sex, but is there more to the poem than an exceptionally deft handling of simultaneous analogy and antithesis? The night scene is not one of complete desolation, for the moon is compared with the elevation of the host; on the other hand, the implications of this are left unexplored. Hugo seems to be using his seabound channel island as a kind of revision of the elements of pastoral. He wants a sinister view of nature, even if peopled by gentle beings, whether the reduction of the poem to statement allows for it or not. Nature satisfies him especially in the harshness of the sea and the rugged island. Quite unlike much of Hugo's earlier nature poetry, many of the pieces written in exile deal with a very real, identifiable landscape and not with conventionalized, literary scenes. As a result, their connotations have some of the ambivalence Hugo felt about his place of exile, which he loved in many ways for its very grimness and inhospitality.

V *Personification*

One poem which seems to be about nature, although it is totally metaphoric, is "O Strophe du poète . . ." ("O Poet's Stanza . . .). This is perhaps generally considered one of the minor pieces in *Les Contemplations,* but it is nevertheless exceptional in its shape and the fact that it deals with imagination, a subject Hugo did not often overtly dwell on. The opening lines involve a picture—rather coy—of nature; the thematic material is similar to passages, which we have not quoted, in "Halte en marchant" and "Pasteurs et Troupeaux":

> O strophe du poète, autrefois dans les fleurs,
> Jetant mille baisers à leurs mille couleurs,
> Tu jouais, et d'avril tu pillais la corbeille ;
> Papillon pour la rose et pour la ruche abeille,
> Tu semais de l'amour et tu faisais du miel ;
> Ton âme bleue était presque mêlée au ciel ;
> Ta robe était d'azur et ton oeil de lumière ;
> Tu criais aux chansons, tes soeurs : Venez ! Chaumière,
> Hameau, ruisseau, forêt, tout chante. L'aube a lui !

(O poet's strophe, once at home among flowers, casting a thousand kisses to their thousand colors, you played and pillaged April's basket. A butterfly for the rose and a bee for the hive, you sowed love and made honey. Your blue soul almost vanished into the sky; your dress was of azure and your eye of light. You cried to your sister songs, "Come! hut, hamlet, brook, forest, all are singing. Dawn has come!")

This personification of the strophe (an awkward term, meant to designate the poet's instrument) as butterfly, bee, and lover, is intended to convey the early pastoral nature of poetry, which, as we

shall see, will change. But the symbolic function of this personification is not realized by the monotonous proliferation of actions,
which merely suggest a cloying sprite. This is a crucial critical problem in Hugo's poetry: his excessive preciosity or false naïveté in
such personifications. We can perhaps point up why these passages
sometimes seem so unsatisfying in Hugo's poetry by considering the
following:

> The Clod and the Pebble
> "Love seeketh not Itself to please,
> Nor for itself hath any care,
> But for another gives its ease,
> And builds a Heaven in Hell's despair."
>
> So sung a little Clod of Clay
> Trodden with the cattle's feet,
> But a Pebble of the brook
> Warbled out these metres meet:
>
> "Love seeketh only Self to please,
> To bind another to Its delight,
> Joys in another's loss of ease,
> And builds a Hell in Heaven's despite."

> The Wild Flower's Song
> As I wander'd the forest,
> The green leaves among,
> I heard a wild flower
> Singing a song:
>
> "I slept in the dark
> In the silent night
> I murmur'd my fears
> And I felt delight.
>
> "In the morning I went
> As rosy as morn
> To seek for new Joy,
> But I met with scorn."

Blake's clod, pebble, and flower speak in verse forms which are
associated with deftness and lightness, whereas Hugo's "strophe du
poète" is imprisoned in a grand meter, the alexandrine, attempting
to express, elephantinely, sprightliness, innocence, and freedom, a
nineteenth-century version of pastoral's Golden Age. The clod and

pebble have a noble sententiousness, the flower a delicate concision; but the speech of Hugo's "strophe" is falsely familiar in tone. Hugo tries for more than this impression at times, but seldom reaches Blake's naturalness. Here he comes closer to it:

> Par-dessus l'horizon aux collines brunies,
> Le soleil, cette fleur des splendeurs infinies,
> Se penchait sur la terre à l'heure du couchant;
> Une humble marguerite, éclose au bord d'un champ,
> Sur un mur gris, croulant parmi l'avoine folle,
> Blanche, épanouissait sa candide auréole;
> Et la petite fleur, par-dessus le vieux mur,
> Regardait fixement dans l'éternel azur
> Le grand astre épanchant sa lumière immortelle.
> —Et moi, j'ai des rayons aussi! lui disait-elle.

("Unité" ["Unity"], Les Contemplations)

(Above the horizon with its darkened hills, the sun, a flower sprung from the infinite splendor, bowed over the earth at its setting. A lowly daisy, flowering at the edge of a field, on a grey wall crumbling amidst the wild oats, spread forth, white and shining, its halo. And the little flower, over the old wall, stared into the eternal blue at the great disk pouring forth its immortal light. "And I have beams, too," the flower said to it.)

It is significant that, despite the immediately preceding example and others comparable, such personifications tend to be most intense and poetically effective in sinister contexts:

> —Laisse-moi.—Non.—O griffe sombre,
> Bouche horrible! ô torture! ô deuil!
> Pourquoi te glisses-tu dans l'ombre
> Par les fentes de mon cercueil?
>
> —Il faut renouveler ma sève,
> O mort, voici le doux été.
> Toute la nature qui rêve,
> Spectre, a besoin de ma beauté!
> . . . .
> Il faut que je pare le voile
> Des vierges au lever du jour,
> Que je respire pour l'étoile,
> Que je rougisse pour l'amour.
>
> Et pendant que l'aube m'arrose,
> Ma racine vers toi descend.
> —Qui donc es-tu?—Je suis la rose.

—Et que veux-tu?—Boire ton sang.
("Sous terre"["Underground"], *Les Quatre Vents de l'esprit*)

("Leave me." "No." "O dark claw, frightful mouth! O torment! O grief!
Why do you slip into the shadow through the cracks in my coffin?" "My sap
must be renewed, O dead one, sweet summer is come. All of dreaming nature,
ghost, needs my beauty. . . . I must adorn the veil of the virgins at dawn; I
must breathe for the star, I must blush for love. And while dawn gives me
drink, my root goes down to you." "Who then are you?" "I am the rose."
"And what do you want?" "To drink your blood.")

To return to "O Strophe . . . ," it is characteristic that, as the mood
darkens, the personification, which is gradually changing, loses its
coy elfin air and acquires a greater beauty:

Et, douce, tu courais et tu riais. Mais lui,
Le sévère habitant de la bleme caverne
Qu'en haut le jour blanchit, qu'en bas rougit l'Averne,
Le poète qu'ont fait avant l'heure vieillard
La douleur dans la vie et le drame dans l'art,
Lui, le chercheur du gouffre obscur, le chasseur d'ombres
Il a levé la tête un jour hors des décombres,
Et t'a saisie au vol dans l'herbe et dans les blés,
Et, malgré tes effrois et tes cris redoublés,
Toute en pleurs, il t'a prise à l'idylle joyeuse;
Il t'a ravie aux champs, à la source, à l'yeuse,
Aux amours dans les bois près des nids palpitants;
Et maintenant, captive et reine en même temps,
Prisonnière au plus noir de son âme profonde,
Parmi les visions qui flottent comme l'onde,
Sous son crâne à la fois céleste et souterrain,
Assise, et t'accoudant sur un trône d'airain,
Voyant dans ta mémoire, ainsi qu'une ombre vaine,
Fuir l'éblouissement du jour et de la pluine,
Par le maître gardée, et calme, et sans espoir,
Tandis que, près de toi, les drames, groupe noir,
Des sombres passions feuillettent le registre,
Tu rêves dans sa nuit, Proserpine sinistre.

(And gently you ran and laughed. But the dour inhabitant of the ghastly
cavern, which the sun whitens from above and the Avernus reddens from
beneath, the poet who before his time has been aged by sorrow in life and
tragedy in art, he, the seeker of the dark chasm, the shadow hunter, looked
up one day out of the ruins and seized you as you flew through the grass and
wheat, and despite your fright and increasing cries took you, weeping, from

your joyful idyll. He snatched you from the fields, the spring, the oak, from lovemaking in the woods by the quivering nests, and now, at once both captive and queen, a prisoner in the depths of his deep black soul, amidst visions floating like waves, beneath his skull, which is both heavenly and subterranean, you are seated, leaning on a bronze throne, seeing in your memory, like an empty ghost, the brilliance of the sun and the plain flee; you are guarded by the master, and calmly, hopelessly, while by you the black group of tragedies leaf through the register of dark passions, you dream in his night like a sinister Proserpina.)

There are a number of admirable things about this poem. The mythological reference is discreetly introduced, emerges gradually, and only seems complete with the last words. The initial relation between the poet and personified strophe is maintained by altering the myth so that the latter dwells in the former's mind, of which the subterranean part of the earth is an analogy. At the same time, the poet's skull is furnished and concrete-seeming. If we tried to work out the analogies of the poem logically and completely, we should find them defective (for example, surface nature has no metaphoric value), but Hugo's art consists in making the transitions between shifting metaphors seem smooth; the mechanics of analogy are concealed. The poem, which merely compares two things, has been transformed into a sophisticated structure without parallel in Hugo's early work.

VI   *"A Théophile Gautier"*

"Halte en marchant," "Pasteurs et Troupeaux," and "O Strophe . . . " all show considerable syntactic elaboration to match their extended images. Very often, however, Hugo chooses the opposite pattern and readily shifts images, which are contained in relatively short sentences. An especially astonishing example of this is "A Théophile Gautier," which commemorates the death of the poet and in which the couplet shapes the syntax in a way reminiscent of seventeenth-century tragic poetry:

> Lorsqu'un vivant nous quitte, ému, je le contemple;
> Car entrer dans la mort, c'est entrer dans le temple
> Et quand un homme meurt, je vois distinctement
> Dans son ascension mon propre avènement.
> Ami, je sens du sort la sombre plénitude;
> J'ai commencé la mort par de la solitude,
> Je vois mon profond soir vaguement s'étoiler,
> Voici l'heure où je vais, moi aussi, m'en aller.

> *Mon fil trop long frissonne et touche presque au glaive;*
> *Le vent qui t'emporta doucement me soulève,*
> *Et je vais suivre ceux qui m'aimaient, moi banni.*
> *Leur oeil fixe m'attire au fond de l'infini.*
> *J'y cours. Ne fermez pas la porte funéraire.*

(When a living man leaves us, I contemplate him with emotion, for entering death is to enter the temple, and, when a man dies, I distinctly see in his rise my own future. Friend, I feel the dark fullness of fate. I have begun death by solitude. I see my deep evening dimly light up with stars. This is the hour when I also shall go. My too long thread quivers and almost touches the blade. The wind which took you off gently lifts me, and I am going to follow those who loved me when I was banished. Their staring eyes draw me to the depths of infinity. I am hurrying. Do not close the funereal door.)

Here Hugo has deliberately chosen to imitate the measured, solemn movement of Neoclassical verse. The beauty of the lines lies in their subtle gradation: the movement from the generalized dead man to the speaker, and, in careful order, the latter's progress toward death—loneliness, night, the hour, the cutting of the thread by the fates which binds him to life, movement away, and the ultimate goal.

The last verse paragraph of "A Théophile Gautier" says, very delicately and through implication, that they, Gautier, the speaker, and others, were the giants of a vanishing heroic age:

> *Passons; car c'est la loi; nul ne peut s'y soustraire;*
> *Tout penche; et ce grand siècle avec tous ses rayons*
> *Entre en cette ombre immense où pâles nous fuyons.*
> *Oh! quel farouche bruit font dans le crépuscule*
> *Les chênes qu'on abat pour le bûcher d'Hercule!*
> *Les chevaux de la mort se mettent à hennir,*
> *Et sont joyeux, car l'âge éclatant va finir;*
> *Ce siècle altier qui sut dompter le vent contraire,*
> *Expire . . .—O Gautier! toi, leur égal et leur frère,*
> *Tu pars après Dumas, Lamartine et Musset.*
> *L'onde antique est tarie où l'on rajeunissait;*
> *Comme il n'est plus de Styx il n'est plus de Jouvence.*
> *Le dur faucheur avec sa large lame avance*
> *Pensif et pas à pas vers le reste du blé;*
> *C'est mon tour; et la nuit emplit mon oeil troublé*
> *Qui, devinant, hélas, l'avenir des colombes,*
> *Pleure sur des berceaux et sourit à des tombes.*

(Let us pass, for that is the law; no one is exempt. Everything is declining, and this great age with all its beams is entering the immense shadow where we palely flee. Oh, what a terrifying noise is made in the twilight by the oak trees being felled for Hercules' pyre! Death's horses are beginning to neigh and are joyful, for this dazzling epoch is about to end. This proud age, which succeeded in taming the adverse winds, is dying. O Gautier! you, their equal and brother, are leaving after Dumas, Lamartine, and Musset. The ancient stream from which rejuvenation came has dried up; as there is no more Styx, there is no more fountain of youth. The harsh reaper with his broad blade moves pensively and slowly toward the rest of the wheat. It is my turn, and night fills my dim eye, which, foreseeing, alas, what the future holds in store for the dovelike newborn, weeps over cradles and smiles at graves.)

Hugo here succeeds at something he had tried perhaps only once before with success: to give mythic dimensions to modern times (as in the memorial poem about his father discussed in Chapter 4). What he could not do for Napoleon's battles in "L'Expiation" he convincingly did for the Romantic battle in art. And his means are essentially the classicizing references which we have seen him use in regard to his father's death and which, entirely different from the rococo mythology of the eighteenth century (more Latin cupids than Greek Achilles), proved still poetically potent.

The lyric patterns we have observed in this chapter all rely on association rather than a logical structure, or on the working out of an image. In this respect, many of Hugo's poems represent a midpoint between traditional lyric patterns and the very free ones of various late nineteenth-century poets; a midpoint because they are in no way obscure in their associative development, but contain at the same time leaps from subject to subject. Not even Baudelaire's verse shows a greater tendency to develop unconstrained by logical sequence. On the contrary, Baudelaire's preference for stanzas over alexandrine couplets tends to encourage strong logical articulations. The point is not that Hugo was a better poet than Baudelaire—he is often prolix where the latter is dense—but that his mastery of certain technical problems, such as the analogy in "O Strophe . . . ," was more innovative. Associative patterns in poetry cannot, any more than imagistic ones, be considered superior to previous conceptions of lyric. However, they were both the structural principles toward which nineteenth-century French verse constantly tended, and one of the most remarkable things about Hugo's poetry was the way it kept moving farther and farther in these directions despite the poetic generation he belonged to.

CHAPTER 8

The Late Novels

I Les Misérables

HUGO had begun *Les Misérables* (1862) under the title of *Les Misères* in the 1840's. The great period of poetic production of the 1850's interrupted work on the novel, but when he returned to it, his sense of purpose was as strong as ever. His enthusiasm for the project was great since he rightly expected it to be the most resounding success of his career. People who never read verse were to devour this enormous novel, and it, of course, could survive translation as poetry hardly could. Some distinguished admirers of his verse like Flaubert and Baudelaire could not stomach it. A new standard for narrative technique and ironic distance in fiction had been set by *Madame Bovary* in 1857, which the coming generation of novelists was to follow; *Les Misérables* had nothing to teach them. Nonetheless, it eclipsed the rest of Hugo's work for the great mass of readers and certainly assured his financial security.

A plot summary will necessarily be very schematic. At the beginning, Jean Valjean, an escaped convict, steals from the saintly bishop who has offered him hospitality and from a child. The origins of Jean's first crime—stealing a loaf of bread—are glimpsed, and the scene changes to Paris in 1817, where Fantine, a seamstress, is abandoned by her lover, entrusts her daughter to the innkeeper Thénardier in a village, and turns to prostitution when she cannot find sufficiently remunerative work to pay for Cosette's keep. The mayor, who is Jean under an assumed identity and grown prosperous, saves her from the police, in the person of Javert, to whom he will surrender on learning that another man has been sent back to prison in his place. We backtrack to the battle of Waterloo, at the end of which Thénardier saves an officer's life. Jean, who has escaped again from prison, takes Cosette under his wing, and the two spend the next years hiding or living inconspicuously in Paris on money Jean had prudently hidden in the days of his wealth. A new character, Marius, is next presented; he breaks with his grandfather at the death of his father, a former officer of Napoleon's army and the one saved by Thénardier. Marius's political education and his love for Cosette, whom he has no more than seen, occupy the next sections. During the Republican insurrection of 1832, Jean, who has resented Marius, carries the wounded young man to safety through the Paris sewers. Javert commits suicide, dazed at his own behavior toward Jean, and Thénardier, to whom Marius is indebted because of his father, gives up his own pursuit of Jean and leaves for America. Cosette and Marius marry; Jean's life story comes to light, and he dies content.

This account leaves out almost countless episodes and the famous figure of Gavroche, the street urchin, but what cannot be readily conveyed and yet gives such a characteristic color to the novel is not so much the number of events as the involved moving back and forth between characters and situations—all within a carefully worked out time scheme—and the abundant digressions on matters of momentary concern to the plot. The battle of Waterloo episode is the most famous of these, partly because of its length and partly because, seen in one light, it has little relevance to the novel. However, Marius's whole awakening to political and social questions is dependent on his and the reader's awareness of the Napoleonic era. Other digressions are not always intended to create a sense of history so much as to give a feeling of a special institution, like the convent where Cosette is placed, or of some peculiarity of Parisian life like argot. The city, in fact, is depicted with particular care for the character of out-of-the-way areas in it. Hugo's own brand of realism assures an elaborate grounding of the novel in place as well as in time.

The digressive pattern of *Les Misérables* is far more prominent than that of *Notre-Dame de Paris*, which is a matter both of length and of the infinitely richer mass of material which Hugo could take from a historical period he himself had lived through. But, as a glance at the immense table of contents shows, the discursive essays are carefully placed to provide variety in the interest and pace of the novel. They do not at all resemble the interminable and seemingly (at a first reading at least) directionless digressions of Balzac's less harmoniously constructed novels; although Hugo's plan was conceived on a very large scale, the details were not neglected. Furthermore, as was the case in *Notre-Dame de Paris,* there is a stylistic unity in the authorial voice whether it be narrating or expounding.

Modern interest in *Les Misérables* has focused both on the genuine elements of realism in it and, more notably, on the thematics of the work. It has often been observed that this story of rehabilitation and social redemption parallels *La Fin de Satan*: It is the exoteric, contemporary, and realist version of the esoteric myth. At the same time, *Les Misérables* contains elements of symbolism, which, for many, counterbalance the slightly unsubstantial quality of the major (but not the minor) figures. The parallelism with *La Fin de Satan* is, as it has been remarked, somewhat imperfect, since the crime which Jean Valjean expiates is a petty one; however, in society's eyes his guilt is nonetheless considerable for having been a convict at all. His redemptory acts are, as it were, penance for crimes of which life in prison had made him capable even though he did not commit them. Hugo manages thus to give some psychological verisimilitude to his character.

Richard B. Grant has noted a goodly number of Christological references in regard to Jean Valjean, since his self-redemption is accomplished through saving others.[1] However, the dominant impression the novel gives is more somber. It is noteworthy that in the first version, *Les Misères*, the landscapes tend to be crepuscular or nocturnal, to reflect a gray and dreary purgatory.[2] Despite the flamboyance of some later additions, much of this tonality survives in *Les Misérables*; it is not a novel in which light or nature in its sumptuousness plays a major role. The Parisian life of Jean Valjean is largely passed in self-claustration, in semihiding. Furthermore, there is a recurrent imagery of the subterranean: An especially striking example of this comes at the beginning of Part III, Book 7, where, under the title of "Mines and Miners," Hugo develops an image of society as a vast underground structure. Human thought and endeavor extend downward beneath the "hovel and marvel" of civilization to the point where good becomes dubious and begins to take on an evil, lurid coloring, as it approaches the ultimate abyss. The Ugolino of humanity, just one of Hugo's references to Dante's descending circles, lies near the bottom, and it is in this milieu of crime that an important central part of *Les Misérables* takes place. But the most important reference to hell is its embodiment in the sewers of Paris, through which Jean Valjean carries Marius, as the ultimate part of his journey through death to resurrection.[3] Like the pane of glass separating man from God in *Notre-Dame de Paris*, there is a grill covering the outlet to the sewers, which Jean Valjean finally makes his way to, but this time salvation takes place—through the ironic intervention of Thénardier, Jean's enemy, who, not recognizing him, opens the locked grating.

II Les Travailleurs de la mer

Les Travailleurs de la mer (1866) differs markedly from *Les Misérables* in its structure. The opening section, "L'Archipel de la Manche" ("The Channel Archipelago"), is devoted to an essay, sociological, historical, and geographic, on the Channel Islands. Much of the material which might otherwise form digressive interludes as in the preceding novel is here gathered together at the beginning, a pattern Balzac had sometimes used. The actual story is very simple. Gilliatt the fisherman has loved from a distance Déruchette, the daughter of a steamship owner. When the boat is wrecked on the rocks, Lethierry offers Déruchette to the man who can salvage the engine, which has remained intact. Gilliatt succeeds, only to find that in the meantime Déruchette has fallen in love with another man. He wishes her well and retreats to a rock, where the tide engulfs him as the newlyweds leave for England.

Grant points out that the story is a paradigm of heroic myth: Gilliatt undergoes a trial and brings back a trophy in triumph. At his death the hero is reabsorbed into nature, in this case the sea.[4] The test, though, of whether we perceive archetypal patterns in an ostensibly contemporary, realistic novel can come only from the effect all manner of details in the texture of the work create. Hugo's novel is very successful in his presentation of Gilliatt's struggle as one with mythic forces. The sea imagery is strongly sexualized, suggesting that the virgin hero is doing far more than merely salvaging an engine, although the latter feat is, in practical terms, no mean one for one man alone. The climax of the battle with the elements is not the actual hoisting of the engine so much as an encounter with evil in the form of a giant octopus. This is, for good reasons, one of the most famous passages in Hugo's fiction. It is lengthy, but I should like to quote just a few sentences to give some idea of the quality of the prose, which even in translation is arresting:

A greyish form quivers in the water. It is as thick as your arm and a half-ell long; it is a rag. This form looks like a closed umbrella without a handle. This scrap moves toward you little by little. Suddenly it opens; eight beams shoot back from a face with two eyes. These beams live. There is a flame in their undulations. It is a kind of wheel. Opened up it is four or five feet in diameter. A hideous flowering. It flings itself on you.

Hugo's later prose uses, especially in heightened moments, the same abrupt parataxis that his visionary poetry often does; in terms of prose style, it might be called an apocalyptic version of the traditional French *style coupé*. Here we recognize the octopus as a variant on Hugo's obsessive image of the spider as fate and death. The embrace of the creature is easily translatable into a fatal sexual act. In this central section of *Les Travailleurs de la mer* Hugo succeeds in gradually moving us into imagery of an anagogical nature, that is, representing good and evil in absolute terms. Gilliatt's battle ends with his having achieved peace through descent into hell and return; he no longer needs worldly goods, and we may interpret his suicide as a natural consequence of his having fulfilled his heroic mission and being no longer needed in the world of men.

III L'Homme qui rit

While *Les Travailleurs de la mer* is generally admired, *L'Homme qui rit* (1869) appeals largely to those who are interested in the basic materials of Hugo's imagination and its archetypes. The setting in late seventeenth-century England tends to be fanciful and the plot outlandish. It is the main figures which attract our attention. Gwynplaine, unbeknowst to himself the son of an exiled lord, has had his mouth slit in childhood by the company of *comprachicos,* who mutilate children to make them display freaks. His grotesque and permanent laugh gives its title to the novel. Abandoned as a boy, he finds an orphaned blind infant, who will be named Déa by the man who takes them in. The latter, Ursus, has a pet wolf named Homo; this upside-down world represents the hiding of natural qualities under a necessary masquerade in a sinister world, just as Gwynplaine's mutilation conceals his true nature. Only Déa stands for what she seems to be. In a strange performance, a "mystery" they support themselves by giving, the wolf and bear-man represent nature, Déa spirit, and Gwynplaine man redeemed, until he turns his face to the crowd and provokes their laughter: Evil triumphs. A depraved aristocrat, Josiane, lures off Gwynplaine to sleep with her, only to lose interest when it is discovered that he is now a lord. After a disastrous appearance in the House of Lords he rejoins Ursus and Déa, who is dying, then commits suicide.

Hugo's interest in abnormalities and mutilation can be found elsewhere in his work, but seldom so prominently. That matter is evil would seem to be the import of the novel: Gwynplaine represents man, Déa soul, and the aristocracy subhuman forces of evil. All manner of accessory symbols contribute to the generally dark mood of the novel, which shows Hugo's imagination in a kind of raw form, from which we can only conclude that it was essentially dualistic with the sinister tending to prevail.

IV *Summing Up*

Hugo's career as a novelist describes a curve: After reaching a peak, it descends again into very minor work. *L'Homme qui rit* is still intriguing because of its extremely overt symbolism, although it could hardly be recommended as skillful in terms of coherence. The last novel, *Quatre-vingt-treize* (1873), which we shall not discuss, deals with the French Revolution and contains more relentless preaching about society than its predecessors. The Revolution, oddly enough, for all its significance in Hugo's mind, never received adequate treatment in his work. This key event in his vision of history somehow always eluded him in his greatest periods of inspiration.

While Hugo's novels do not belong to the mainstream of French fiction, *Notre-Dame de Paris* perhaps excepted, the virtues of the later ones are probably more apparent to the discriminating reader today than they were to Flaubert and Baudelaire. Enough kinds of fiction have been written since then—including, notably, the revival of Gothic devices in recent Anglo-American literature— that we are more willing to accept the bizarre qualities of Hugo's work and the fact of a plurality of possible techniques than was possible during the rise of the great Realist tradition in France. Digressive patterns and overtly symbolic characters in particular do not offend as they once did. And finally, Hugo's stylistic inventiveness stands out as the remarkable achievement it was.

CHAPTER 9

Conclusion

I *Poetics and Poetic Lineage*

HUGO'S conception of poetry is interestingly suggested here and there in "But de cette publication" ("Purpose of this Publication") from *Littérature et Philosophie mêlées*, a collection of essays which appeared in 1834. More so in some ways than in his prefaces, especially that of *Cromwell*, we find in this piece a balanced picture of Hugo's early mature reflections on his art. All poetry begins in questions of form, language, and style, and the state of language at the time of a poet's beginnings can be favorable, as during the Baroque period, or unpropitious, as after Racine. Form cannot be separated from idea, expression from content. Hugo steers clearly away from all emotional fallacies about the nature of art and goes beyond the often superficial (if essential) distinction between the Romantic and the Classic. He focuses attention on the materials of poetry: It is not surprising that unlike Lamartine, Vigny, or Musset, his poetry of the 1830's never shows a disparity between conception and execution. His verbal instrument was indeed inseparable from his ideas, and he did not undertake, before he was ready for it as a craftsman, one of those ambitious and botched great philosophical poems so many of his contemporaries did, as H. J. Hunt's book shows.

To this postemotive, nonrhetorical theory of art, so different from those current in France in the late eighteenth and early nineteenth centuries, Hugo joined what René Wellek calls a dialectical theory of art: the reconciliation of contrasts as represented by the theory of the grotesque.[1] This is opposed to the Neoclassical taste for unity of tone and surface. While Hugo stated his notions on the grotesque in respect to drama primarily, he included more than stage plays in the term *drame*. We can extend this theory to his lyric collections insofar as similar effects of reconciliation may be found in them. Hugo's place in critical theorizing about art is therefore not negligible, and it has even been said that "with Hugo there emerges in France for the first time a concept of poetry which can be defined as symbolistic and dialectical."[2] That Hugo's poetry is "symbolistic" is true in a double sense: His contemporaries of the 1830's were impressed by many symbols that we would tend to call allegorical, and, later in his career, Hugo evolved a more elaborate symbolic language.

The social dimension of art is a question Hugo dealt with in a somewhat gingerly fashion as befits its complexity. At the time he spoke of pure poetry, he was opposed to a kind of relentlessly moralizing criticism. That art had some civilizing value he was not about to reject, however, and the formula that art has no *direct* usefulness became his ("But de cette publication"). In later years, at the time when *l'art pour l'art* had become an established phrase and concept, he felt obliged to affirm that art serves truth ("Le Beau serviteur du vrai" ["Beauty the Servant of Truth"] in *William Shakespeare,* 1864), which is a way around the question of what art is for by proclaiming what art is. But Hugo was to make a further leap in theory in the posthumous *Promontorium Somnii* (dating from the 1860's like *William Shakespeare*), where he takes up the term that the symbolists were to prefer above all others in discussions of art: dream *(rêve)*. Rather than "imagination," which had had in any case a somewhat limited use in French aesthetics, *rêve* suggests a greater and even potentially dangerous source of the mind's activities: "Man needs dreams," but these dreams include the most irrational flights of religion and philosophy as well as the source of poetry. Given Hugo's penchant for the sinister, his choice of terms is not altogether surprising.

That art can serve both truth and dreams is a paradox only on the surface, since dreams bring forth the great unconscious archetypes which constitute truth, and here again Hugo's theory of literature is remarkably advanced. The nature of greatness in literature is, more so than the English poet, the subject of *William Shakespeare,* and in it Hugo constructs a kind of literary genealogy for himself. The archetypical writers are presented one by one and joined by their common concern for terrifying visions; Job, Aeschylus, Isaiah, Ezekiel, Juvenal, Tacitus, Saint John, Saint Paul, and Dante constitute the main line of them, with Homer, Lucretius, Rabelais, Cervantes, and Shakespeare seeming to be included more out of piety than passionate conviction. Hugo sees the biblical writers, Aeschylus, the Silver Age Romans, and Dante as forming a natural lineage for his own visionary poetry. At times, he seems almost to forget the reality of these writers in imposing on them his own vision. Of Job he says that the sun in it is sinister. There are, in fact, no solar images in Job, the most frequent ones being of darkness, dust, wind, and shadow. Dante is not the allegorical poet of the three realms, since after the *Inferno* he ceases to be interesting: Only those aspects of Dante which can be assimilated to the prophets count. Basically, Hugo is trying to see the warning, castigating figure of the biblical poets as the central line of world literature.

The role that the Bible played in Hugo's life as source and as self-justification demonstrates an important fact about French Romantic poets, of whom Hugo is both the characteristic and the towering figure. The Romantic love of myth, which in England turned poets back to the achievements of the pre-Neoclassical period, could not in France find a viable national tradition. Instead, the Bible became their great source book. Lamartine's Jobian "Novissima verba" and *La Chute d'un ange,* suggested by a line of Genesis, Vigny's reworking of the stories of Moses, Samson, and the gospel, Nerval's dying Christ, all owe their origins to the central place the Bible came to occupy in French Romanticism. Sometimes, of course, biblical material was mediated by religious tradition: Gautier's and Musset's anguish over the end of Christianity is not biblical in origin, but belongs to the climate of thought of their times. Hugo was the fullest user of the Bible of all the French Romantics, the least influenced by simple religious tradition, and in that way is the exemplary figure of this tendency in French literature. And it is significant that of all the books of the Bible, the one to leave the deepest trace in his work is the somewhat unorthodox-seeming Job, which Hugo understood to be "the most ancient Arabic poem."

II *"Le Verbe"*

Car le mot qu'on le sache, est un être vivant.
. . . .
Il est vie, esprit, germe, ouragan, vertu, feu;
Car le mot, c'est le Verbe, et le Verbe, c'est Dieu.
("Réponse à un acte d'accusation—suite," *Les Contemplations*)

(For the word, you should know, is a living creature. . . . It is life, mind, seed, storm, potential, fire; for the word is the Logos, and the Logos is God.)

French distinguishes Saint John's logos from ordinary speech as "le Verbe," and beginning with Hugo the use of the term in French poetics suggests a special attitude toward language. It envisages language as creative, incantatory, anterior, and superior to things. We expect such language to move in patterns independent from common reality, to remake the world, or be the vehicle of myth. Not all poetic language is of this kind; many dramatic lyrics try to render as closely as possible situations, men and women, things. I am reminded of the remarks T. S. Eliot made about Swinburne's poetic language, which are all the more suggestive in the light of Swinburne's utter worship of Hugo. Eliot emphasized the vastness of Swinburne's work and the peculiar fact that no particular poem represents him at his absolute best and is indispensable. "His diffuseness is one of his glories."[3] Much the same might be said of Hugo, who never put the quintessence of his genius into a single poem. That there is little material for so much verse might also be observed of parts of *Dieu*, the longer poems in *Les Contemplations*, or of "Le Satyre." Finally, the distance of the verbal texture from any historically real object is brought up and denounced by Eliot. The denunciation is a sound one, but it fails to take into account a whole current of poetry in which the hypnotic repetition of verbal patterns, with a minimum of developmental movement, not only obtains but is powerful in its effect. The verses of the biblical poets come first to mind; the beauty of the lines obscures for most readers the exact references in their historical time. An incantatory, mythic kind of verse recurs in the Romantic period; parts of Blake and Novalis are among its examples.

"Working words" is a second major charge made by Eliot in regard to Swinburne and which we should take note of, for although Hugo was incomparably the greater poet, Swinburne's mannerisms are not unrelated to the older poet's persistent and peculiar handling of many terms. Recurrent adjectives such as *sombre, obscur, sinistre, formidable, âpre, blême, difforme,* and so forth are commonly used where we would not necessarily expect them, and create a kind of symbolic dimension of meaning. There are also other forms of private rhetoric: the ghostly verbal nouns (*arrachements*), the plural of abstract nouns (*passages de méduses*), and color adjectives used peculiarly (*fauve* [meaning "wild" not "tawny"], *vermeil* ["golden" not "vermilion"]). Here and there etymological meanings obtrude in a way which is not common in French Romantic poetry: *candide* means "white," *splendide* "shining," *émouvoir* "move." In syntax there are two superconcise formulas: the double noun (*oeil flambeau, pâtre promontoire*) and abrupt copulae (*Satan est une lyre ainsi que Gabriel*). In the rhetorical domain still, there are marvelous transfers of epithet: *sueur résignée*. Finally, the antithesis for which Hugo is famous lends itself especially well to incantatory language.

One of the most curious developments in Hugo's working of words—and most significant for the limitations of his poetry—is the way in which he sometimes uses the same cast of diction for radically different situations. There is a fascinating example of this in *Toute la lyre*, which Michael Riffaterre points out;[4] the diction of the "Hors de la terre" sections of *La Fin de Satan* is used to describe the relatively minor unpleasantness Hugo encountered in public life:

> *Le fauve acharnement de la haine est sur toi.*
> *Toi qui jadis planais archange, et qu'une loi*
> *Met sur la terre, au fond des visions funèbres,*
> *Prisonnier dans la cage énorme des ténèbres,*
> *Toi, l'aigle échevelé de l'ombre, le banni*
> *Tombé d'un infini dans un autre infini,*
> *Du zénith dans l'abîme et du ciel dans ton âme,*
> *Eclairé, mais brûlé par ta profonde flamme,*
> *Rongé du noir regret du firmament vermeil,*
> *Toi dont l'oeil fixe fait un reproche au soleil*
> *Et semble demander de quel droit l'on t'exile,*
> *Toi qui n'as plus que toi pour cime et pour asile,*
> *Tu ne te distrais point de ton rêve éternel.*   (V, 36)

(The wild determination of hate is against you. O you, who once soared like an archangel and whom a law places on earth in the depths of funereal visions, a prisoner in the enormous cage of darkness, you, the ruffled eagle of shadow, the exile fallen from one infinity into another, from the zenith into the abyss, from heaven into your soul, you, illuminated but burned by your deep flame, gnawed by black longing for the golden sky, you, whose staring eye is a reproach to the sun and seems to ask by what right you are exiled, you, who now have only yourself for apogee and asylum, you cannot be turned away from your eternal dream.)

The verbal system of this passage of 1874 hardly differs from that of the epic of Satan; the mechanisms of Hugo's language are at work almost without regard to the "object," as Eliot would have put it. The capacities for fabricating beautiful but somewhat empty verbiage are a distinct poetic danger for a great mythmaker like Hugo. The same syncretic way of thinking which led him to try to make of Napoleon a legendary figure, while, as Baudelaire pointed out, he was merely a historical one, here causes Hugo to invest the trivial with portentous meaning. Sometimes this works, as in many of the poems about the Channel Islands in *Les Contemplations;* elsewhere, the reader is merely uncomfortably aware of a disparity between the subject and the extraordinary verbal means deployed.

If, on the one hand, we observe a profusion of sheer rhetoric, of "verbalism" in Hugo, we must recall at the same time how frequently his figurative language grows out of real scenes, out of a concrete basis. The shepherd-headland of "Pasteurs et Troupeaux" is an example, as well as the numerous shifts from literal to metaphoric we have noted as early as *Les Orientales.* The figures are structural and not decorative. Furthermore, the sources of Hugo's metaphors can be exceptionally broad and significantly include the low or commonplace. The images we noted in *Châtiments* are exemplary in this respect. In short, the gift for seeing the concrete balances Hugo's tendency toward verbal excess. However, if the antithetical, incantatory style is only one aspect of Hugo's poetry, it is the one which in many respects seems the most modern, the most original for his day. Poets as different as Claudel, Saint-John Perse, and the Surrealists have shown a similar tendency to build up verbal mirages. In this way, Hugo's poetry bridges the gap between more conventional sides of French Romanticism and the successive waves of modernist invention which followed. This is the quality in Hugo which his contemporaries largely ignored, but it is the one which now makes his place in nineteenth-century French poetry seem even more imposing in some ways than it once did. We tend today to look in Romantic poetry not so much for the *sensibilité* the nineteenth century, after the eighteenth, prized, but rather for the gift of mythmaking, of creating a powerful verbal world which seems complete in itself. It was not, by and large, given to the French Romantics to achieve this, even though they glimpsed it, but Hugo was the great exception, which makes his verse different in kind, not just in quality, from that of most of his contemporaries.

III *Influence*

"When you think of what French poetry was before he appeared and what a rejuvenation it has undergone since his arrival, when you imagine how insignificant it would have been if he had not appeared, how many deep and mysterious feelings which have been put into words would have remained unexpressed, how many intelligent minds he has brought into being, how many men who have shone because of him and would otherwise have remained obscure, it is impossible not to consider him as one of those rare and providential minds who in the domain of literature bring about the salvation of us all. . ." The words are Baudelaire's in his 1861 essay on Hugo, which attempts some kind of general judgment. Although, as Baudelaire indicates, the influence of Hugo on nineteenth-century French poetry was deep and pervasive, it is not always an easy one to demonstrate. Some of it was exerted at secondhand, as through Gautier, who was perhaps the most obvious influence on Baudelaire himself; another side of it is highly technical and can best be judged by the fact that Théodore de Banville in his *Petit Traité de poésie française* refers the reader to Hugo's practice as representing the height of prosodic achievement. Baudelaire goes on in his essay to stress the descriptive and analogical virtues of Hugo's poetry, which are among the easiest to perceive in their action on other poets, since they can be clearly dated from *Les Orientales,* at a time when no other poet's work offered such abundant examples of them. These are the qualities that a less than major but highly influential poet such as Leconte de Lisle could absorb and pass on.

The use Mallarmé made of Hugo has been investigated to any depth only fairly recently.[5] The passing influence of Baudelaire obscured it, and, while Hugo and Mallarmé were essentially very dissimilar poets, the latter was extremely susceptible to bookish influence and to Hugo's *trouvailles* of style. The case of Rimbaud is quite different, however, because, never so deeply influenced by Baudelaire, the derivation of his style from Hugo's remained clearer during a greater part of his work. *Châtiments,* with its often violent tone and imagery, seems to have made a particular impression on Rimbaud, and his poems dealing with the fall of the Second Empire not surprisingly reflect this.

With Mallarmé, Rimbaud, and Verlaine, however, the need for Hugo's example declined, since, in the very domain of inventive imagery by which he had so long dominated French poetry, they found new, unexplored paths, and Mallarmé and Rimbaud were also mythmakers in their own right. While Hugo ceased to be relevant to poets, his reputation was established in academic circles, and soon a selection of his verse became customary in the curriculum. This was inevitable but hardly advantageous to Hugo's image as a dominant figure in French literature, since the poems which came to represent his work were not among the most adventurous; study of *La Fin de Satan, Dieu,* and the apocalyptic poems scattered elsewhere in his work received little place. It has taken decades to reverse the notion of Hugo as a primarily sentimental, convention-ridden Romantic, who could not bear comparison with his most important contemporaries in English and German—his *oeuvre* was simply too vast to be absorbed and digested; he wrote too much that was nonessential. Now, tentatively, we can revise earlier judgments of him and see how important his poetry is to French literature and to nineteenth-century poetry as a whole.

Notes and References

Chapter One

1. Charles Baudouin, *Psychanalyse de Victor Hugo.*
2. See, however, Robert E. Turner, *The Sixteenth Century in Victor Hugo's Inspiration.*
3. Sec Richard B. Grant, *The Perilous Quest,* pp. 6–17.
4. See Maurice Bardèche, *Balzac Romancier* (Paris: Plon, 1941), especially pp. 1–41.

Chapter Two

1 For more details see Michael Riffaterre, *Essais de stylistique structurale,* pp. 242–58.
2. The second preface (1832) is especially important.
3. See Charles Baudouin, *Psychanalyse de Victor Hugo,* pp. 127–48.
4. See Richard B. Grant, *The Perilous Quest,* pp. 53–71.

Chapter Three

1. See Richard B. Grant, *The Perilous Quest,* pp. 79–83.
2. See Jean-Bertrand Barrère, *Hugo: L'Homme et l'Oeuvre,* p. 88.
3. Sec Charles Baudouin, *Psychanalyse de Victor Hugo,* pp. 42–44.
4. For a more thorough exploration of mythic archetypes in *Les Burgraves,* see Richard B. Grant, *The Perilous Quest,* pp. 107–21.

Chapter Four

1. See A. Guiard, *Virgile et Victor Hugo,* and Jean Gaudon, *Le Temps de la contemplation,* pp. 54–75.
2. See Jean Gaudon, *Le Temps de la contemplation,* pp. 76–88.

Chapter Five

1. See Herbert J. Hunt, *The Epic in Nineteenth-Century France.*
2. *Ibid.,* pp. 146–48.
3. See Denis Saurat, *Victor Hugo et les Dieux du peuple,* pp. 66–67.
4. See René Journet and Guy Robert, *Notes sur "Les Contemplations,"* pp. 312–17.
5. Jean Gaudon, *Ce que disent les tables parlantes,* pp. 54–55.

6. For an excellent résumé of the question, see *Les Contemplations,* ed. Léon Cellier, pp. 778–81.

7. See René Journet and Guy Robert, *Notes sur "Les Contemplations,"* pp. 218–20.

8. See Denis Saurat, *Victor Hugo et les Dieux du peuple,* pp. 79–80.

9. *Ibid.,* pp. 20–32.

10. See *Les Contemplations,* ed. Léon Cellier, pp. 793–94.

11. The titles of the two parts of *Dieu* vary in manuscript as well as in editions. The part we have just alluded to, which was the first to be written and generally placed second, has occasionally been called "Ascension dans les ténèbres" ("Ascension into Darkness") as well, although the latter title has also been given to the second of the two parts to have been written. The latter is often subdivided into "L'Esprit humain" ("The Human Mind") and "Les Voix" ("The Voices"). We shall use the titles given in the definitive critical edition, that of René Journet and Guy Robert, in which the 1855 part is called *Dieu (L'Océan d'en haut)* and the 1856 section *Dieu (Le Seuil du gouffre).*

12. See Jean Gaudon, *Ce que disent les tables parlantes,* p. 94.

13. *Ibid.,* pp. 98–99.

14. *Dieu (L'Océan d'en haut),* ed. René Journet and Guy Robert, pp. 180–81.

15. See *Dieu (Le Seuil du gouffre),* ed. René Journet and Guy Robert, p. 144.

16. See *L'Ane,* ed. Pierre Albouy, pp. 11–60.

Chapter Six

1. See Denis Saurat, *Victor Hugo et les Dieux du peuple,* pp. 71–72.

2. See Naomi Schor, "Superposition of Models in *La Légende des siècles,*" *Romanic Review* 65, January, 1974.

3. *Ibid.*

4. The idea of the Satyr-Pan-All seems to come from a few lines of Moreri. See Jean Gaudon, *Le Temps de la contemplation,* p. 376. Pan and *pan* meaning all is a traditional play on words.

5. See Richard B. Grant, *The Perilous Quest,* pp. 138–39.

6. These plays are varied in inspiration. Those not included in other collections were posthumously published as *Le Théatre en liberté.*

7. Algernon Charles Swinburne, *A Study of Victor Hugo,* p. 102.

Chapter Eight

1. See all of Grant's important chapter, *The Perilous Quest,* pp. 154–76.

2. See Jean Gaudon, *Le Temps de la contemplation,* pp. 136–42.

3. See Victor Brombert, "Victor Hugo, la prison et l'espace," *Revue des Sciences Humaines,* January-March, 1965.

4. See Richard B. Grant, *The Perilous Quest,* pp. 177–98.

Chapter Nine

1. René Wellek, *The Romantic Age,* p. 255.

2. *Ibid.,* p. 3.

3. T.S. Eliot, *Selected Essays* (New York: Harcourt Brace, 1932), p. 282.

4. See Michael Riffaterre, *Essais de stylistique structurale,* pp. 208–15.

5. See Antoine Fongaro, "Mallarmé et Victor Hugo," *Revue des Sciences Humaines,* October-December, 1965.

Selected Bibliography

PRIMARY SOURCES

Oeuvres complètes, ed. Paul Meurice, Gustave Simon, Cécile Daubray, 45 vols. Paris: Imprimerie Nationale, 1904–1952. In the absence of critical editions of quality, this remains the basic text for Hugo's works.

L'Ane, ed. Pierre Albouy. Paris: Flammarion, 1966.

Châtiments, ed. Paul Berret, 2 vols. Paris: Grand Ecrivains de France, Hachette, 1932. Still useful.

Choix de poèmes, ed. Jean Gaudon. Manchester, England: Manchester University Press, 1957.

Les Contemplations, ed. Léon Cellier. Paris: Garnier, 1969. A remarkable edition.

Les Contemplations, ed. Joseph Vianey. Paris: Grands Ecrivains de France, Hachette, 1922. Still useful.

Dieu (fragments), ed. René Journet and Guy Robert. Paris: Flammarion, 1969. Definitive.

Dieu (L'Océan d'en haut), ed. René Journet and Guy Robert. Paris: Nizet, 1960. Definitive.

Dieu (Le Seuil du gouffre), ed. René Journet and Guy Robert. Paris: Nizet, 1961. Definitive.

La Légende des siècles, ed. Paul Berret, 6 vols. Paris: Grands Ecrivains de France, Hachette, 1920–1927. This edition, the most thorough one, presents the three series separately rather than the collective edition.

La Légende des siècles, La Fin de Satan, Dieu, ed. Jacques Truchet. Paris: Pléiade, Gallimard, 1950. The edition of *La Légende* is adequate, that of *La Fin de Satan* the most easily available one, and that of *Dieu* completely inadequate compared with the Journet-Robert edition.

Mangeront-ils?, ed. René Journet and Guy Robert. Paris: Flammarion, 1970. The most lyrical of the plays in *Le Théâtre en liberté.*

Les Orientales, ed. Elizabeth Barineau, 2 vols. Paris: Didier, 1952.

Oeuvres poétiques, ed. Pierre Albouy, I. *Avant l'exil,* II. *Châtiments, Les Contemplations.* Paris: Pléiade, Gallimard, 1964 and 1967. The best edition for the volumes of the 1830's, very usable for *Châtiments,* but far inferior to the Cellier edition for *Les Contemplations.*

Post-Scriptum de ma vie, ed. Henri Guillemin. Neuchatel: Ides et Calendes, 1961. Curious jottings.

La Préface de Cromwell, ed. Maurice Souriau. Paris: Société française d'Imprimerie, n.d.

Promontorium Somnii, ed. René Journet and Guy Robert. Paris: Les Belles Lettres, 1961. From the *reliquat* of *William Shakespeare.*

Ruy Blas, ed. Anne Ubersfeld, Vol. 1. Paris: Les Belles Lettres, 1971.
Théâtre complet, ed. J. J. Thierry and Josette Mélèze, 2 vols. Paris: Pléiade,
  Gallimard, 1963–1964. Easily available but negligible as an edition.

SECONDARY SOURCES

A certain number of older works whose conclusions are embodied in more
recent ones have been omitted.

ALBOUY, PIERRE. *La Création mythologique chez Victor Hugo.* Paris: José
  Corti, 1963. Very rich in detail, but poor on the theory of myth.
BARRÈRE, JEAN-BERTRAND. *La Fantaisie de Victor Hugo,* 3 vols. Paris: José
  Corti, 1949–1960. Hugo's "fantasy" as opposed to imagination.
———*Victor Hugo: L'Homme et l'Oeuvre.* Paris: Boivin, 1952. Indispens-
  able.
BAUDOUIN, CHARLES. *Psychanalyse de Victor Hugo.* Geneva: Editions du
  Mont-Blanc, 1943. Fascinating study of themes and images.
BAUER, HENRI FRANÇOIS. *Les "Ballades" de Victor Hugo.* Paris: Presses
  Modernes, 1935. Useful for early Romanticism.
BROMBERT, VICTOR. "Victor Hugo, la prison et l'espace." *Revue des Sciences
  Humaines,* nouvelle série, fasc. 117, January-March, 1965, pp. 59 79.
  Extremely rich thematic study.
CHAHINE, SAMIA. *La Dramaturgie de Victor Hugo (1816–43).* Paris: Nizet,
  1971. Terminology often confusing, but touches on all the main
  problems
FONGARO, ANTOINE. "Mallarmé et Hugo." *Revue des Sciences Humaines,*
  nouvelle série, fasc. 120, October-December, 1965, pp. 515–27. Very
  revealing study.
GAUDON, JEAN. *Ce que disent les tables parlantes: Victor Hugo à Jersey.*
  Paris: Pauvert, 1964. Contains some new material,
———*Le Temps de la contemplation: L'Oeuvre poétique de Victor Hugo
  des "Misères" au "Seuil du gouffre."* Paris: Flammarion, 1969. A
  vast study of themes and images.
GRANT, RICHARD B. *The Perilous Quest: Image, Myth and Prophecy in
  the Narratives of Victor Hugo.* Durham, N.C.: Duke University Press,
  1968. Essential for narrative works.
GRILLET, CLAUDIUS. *La Bible dans Victor Hugo.* Lyon: Vitte, 1910. Sound
  treatment of essentials. Neither letter nor spirit receives its due.
GUIARD, AMÉDÉE. *Virgile et Victor Hugo.* Paris: Bloud, 1910. Sound
  treatment of essentials. Mechanical.
HOUSTON, JOHN PORTER. *The Demonic Imagination: Style and Theme in
  French Romantic Poetry.* Baton Rouge: Louisiana State University
  Press, 1969. Structure of Hugo's demonic imagery and its relation to
  other Romantic poets.
HUNT, HERBERT J. *The Epic in Nineteenth-Century France.* Oxford: Black-

well, 1941. Invaluable for the background of Hugo's most ambitious poetic efforts.

JOURNET, RENÉ, and GUY B. ROBERT. *Notes sur "Les Contemplations."* Paris: Les Belles Lettres, 1958. Important stylistic commentary as well as other valuable information.

LEVAILLANT, MAURICE. *La Crise mystique de Victor Hugo.* Paris: José Corti, 1954. On Hugo's state of mind in the 1850's.

MAILLON, JEAN. *Victor Hugo et l'art architectural.* Paris: Presses Universitaires de France, 1962. A thorough study.

MAUROIS, ANDRÉ. *Olympio ou la vie de Victor Hugo.* Paris: Hachette, 1954. The best biography, scholarly and readable.

PIROUÉ, GEORGES. *Victor Hugo romancier ou les dessus de l'inconnu.* Paris: Denoël, 1964. An attempt at reevaluation.

POULET, GEORGES. *La Distance intérieure.* Paris: Plon, 1952. Contains a very important essay on Hugo's spatial imagery.

PY, ALBERT. *Les Mythes grecs dans la poésie de Victor Hugo.* Geneva: Droz, 1963. A useful survey.

RIFFATERRE, MICHAEL. *Essais de stylistique structurale.* Paris: Flammarion, 1971. Important essays on *Les Orientales* and recurrent verbal patterns.

ROCHETTE, AUGUSTE. *L'Alexandrin chez Victor Hugo.* Paris: Hachette, 1911. Exhaustive and for specialists only, but essential in parts.

ROOS, JACQUES. *Les Idées philosophiques de Victor Hugo.* Paris: Nizet, 1958. Hugo and Ballanche; one of the more recent attempts to find sources for Hugo's thought.

SAURAT, DENIS. *Victor Hugo et les Dieux du peuple.* Paris: La Colombe, 1948. Hugo and the Cabala: fascinating and much criticized.

SCHOR, NAOMI. "Superposition of Models in *La Légende des siècles*." *Romanic Review*, 65, January, 1974, pp. 42–51.

SIMON, GUSTAVE. *Les Tables tournantes de Jersey.* Paris: Conard, 1923. The transcript of the seances, to be supplemented by JEAN GAUDON, *Ce que disent.*

SWINBURNE, ALGERNON CHARLES. *A Study of Victor Hugo.* London: Chatto and Windus, 1886. Fascinating for what one important poet finds in another.

TURNER, ROBERT E. *The Sixteenth Century in Victor Hugo's Inspiration.* New York: Columbia University Press, 1934. Workmanlike.

VAN TIEGHEM, PHILIPPE. *Dictionnaire de Victor Hugo.* Paris: Larousse, 1970. Useful but with inexplicable omissions.

VIATTE, AUGUSTE. *Victor Hugo et les illuminés de son temps.* Montreal: Editions de l'Arbre, 1942. Suggests the complexity of the problem of tracing exact influences.

WELLEK, RENÉ. *The Romantic Age.* Vol. II of *A History of Modern Criticism 1750–1950.* New Haven: Yale University Press, 1955. Contains a valuable analysis of Hugo's literary theories in relation to the larger picture of European Romanticism.

Index